THE MARVELOUS LAND OF OZ

WITHDRAWN

MARVELOUS LAND OF OZ. Contains material originally published in magazine form as THE MARVELOUS LAND OF OZ #1-8. First printing 2012. ISBN# 978-0-7851-6365-7. Published by MARVEL WORLDWIDE, INC., a subsidiary of ENTERTAINMENT, LLC. OFFICE OF PUBLICATION: 135 West 50th Street, New York, NY 10020. Copyright © 2009, 2010 and 2012 Marvel Characters, Inc. All rights reserved. $24.99 per copy in the U.S. and $27.99 in Canada (GST #2852); Canadian Agreement #40668537. All characters featured in this issue and the distinctive names and likenesses thereof, and all related indicia are trademarks of Marvel Characters, Inc. No similarity between any of the names, ers, persons, and/or institutions in this magazine with those of any living or dead person or institution is intended, and any such similarity which may exist is purely coincidental. **Printed in the U.S.A.** ALAN FINE, EVP - Office of the t, Marvel Worldwide, Inc. and EVP & CMO Marvel Characters B.V.; DAN BUCKLEY, Publisher & President - Print, Animation & Digital Divisions; JOE QUESADA, Chief Creative Officer; TOM BREVOORT, SVP of Publishing; DAVID BOGART, perations & Procurement, Publishing; RUWAN JAYATILLEKE, SVP & Associate Publisher, Publishing; C.B. CEBULSKI, SVP of Creator & Content Development; DAVID GABRIEL, SVP of Publishing Sales & Circulation; MICHAEL PASCIULLO, rand Planning & Communications; JIM O'KEEFE, VP of Operations & Logistics; DAN CARR, Executive Director of Publishing Technology; SUSAN CRESPI, Editorial Operations Manager; ALEX MORALES, Publishing Operations Manager; .E., Chairman Emeritus. For information regarding advertising in Marvel Comics or on Marvel.com, please contact Niza Disla, Director of Marvel Partnerships, at ndisla@marvel.com. For Marvel subscription inquiries, please call 800-»8. **Manufactured between 10/3/2012 and 11/5/2012 by R.R. DONNELLEY, INC., SALEM, VA, USA.**

6 5 4 3 2 1

THE MARVELOUS LAND OF OZ

ADAPTED FROM THE NOVEL BY L. FRANK BAUM

Writer: **ERIC SHANOWER**
Artist: **SKOTTIE YOUNG**
Colorist: **JEAN-FRANCOIS BEAULIEU**
Letterer: **JEFF ECKLEBERRY**

Assistant Editor: **MICHAEL HORWITZ**
Editor: **NATE COSBY**

Collection Editor: **MARK D. BEAZLEY**
Assistant Editors: **ALEX STARBUCK & NELSON RIBEIRO**
Editor, Special Projects: **JENNIFER GRÜNWALD**
Senior Editor, Special Projects: **JEFF YOUNGQUIST**
Senior Vice President of Sales: **DAVID GABRIEL**
Production: **JERRY KALINOWSKI**
Book Design: **ARLENE SO**

Editor in Chief: **AXEL ALONSO**
Chief Creative Officer: **JOE QUESADA**
Publisher: **DAN BUCKLEY**
Executive Producer: **ALAN FINE**

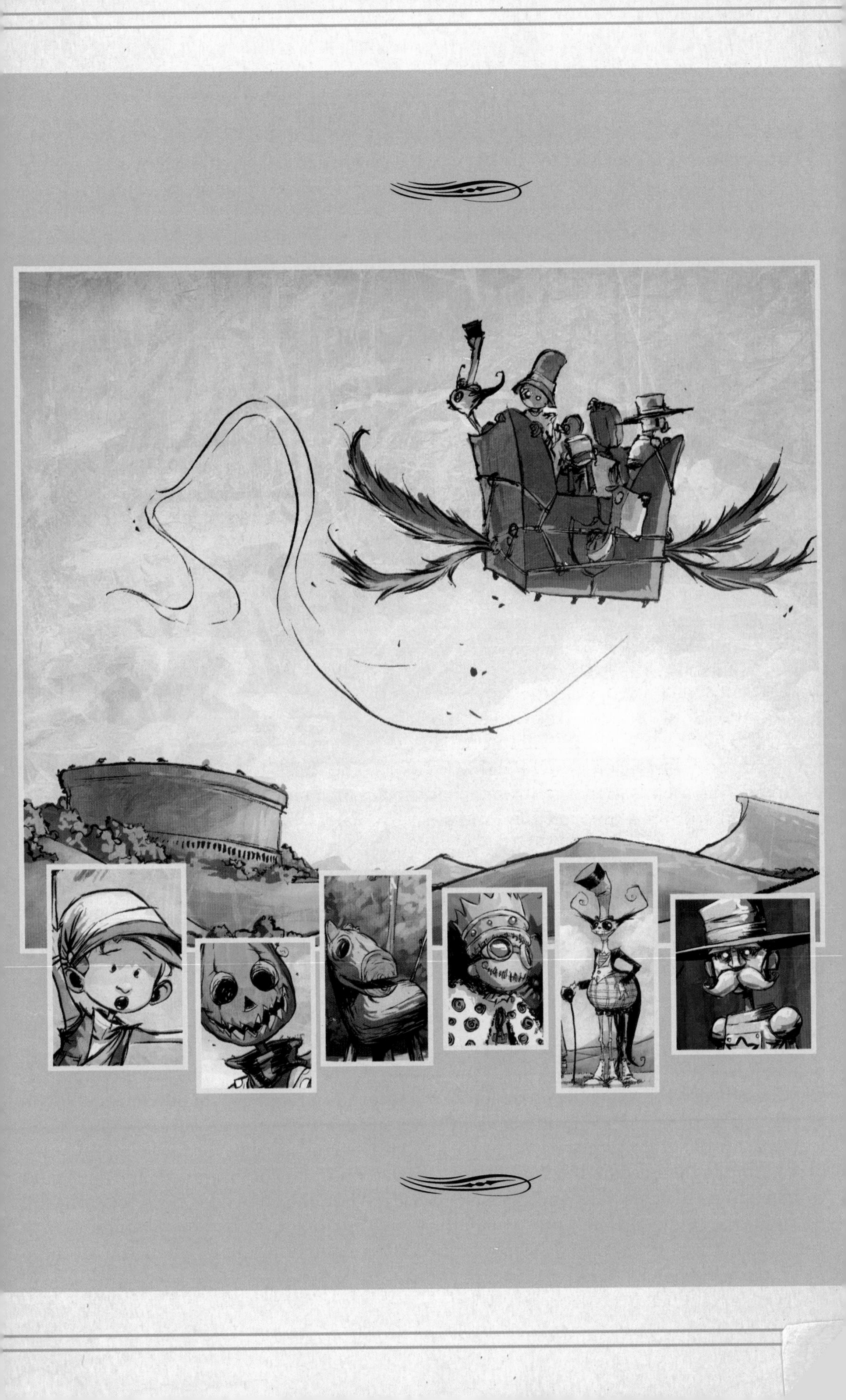

Counting by Twos

For anyone who ever wanted to know what happened to the characters after the end of *The Wonderful Wizard of Oz*, I bring good news—here are more adventures in *The Marvelous Land of Oz*. And the good news continues—this is only the beginning. Oz author L. Frank Baum wrote fourteen full-length Oz books as well as a slew of shorter Oz stories. Other writers continued the series after Baum's death until there were forty Oz books in the official series.

In this sequel to *The Wonderful Wizard of Oz*, the Scarecrow and the Tin Woodman are back. Dorothy Gale and the Cowardly Lion, however, aren't in *The Marvelous Land of Oz*. You'll have to wait for the next Oz story to find out what happens to them.

Instead of Dorothy from Kansas, *The Marvelous Land of Oz* features a boy named Tippetarius, who's usually called Tip. Tip isn't from Kansas or anywhere else in our Great Outside World. He's lived all his life in the Land of Oz. You might think Tip is lucky to live in Oz, but he's actually unlucky enough to live with an old woman named Mombi. Mombi looks like a witch, acts like a witch, and has enough magical powers for a dozen witches. But she refuses to call herself a witch. The reason Tip lives with Mombi is one of the most surprising secrets in all of American children's literature. Don't worry, I wouldn't dream of revealing the secret here. You'll have to read the story to discover it.

At the end of *The Wonderful Wizard of Oz*, the Scarecrow was declared the ruler of the Emerald City. As *The Marvelous Land of Oz* begins, he's doing his best to rule his people using the brains given to him by the Wizard. Likewise, the Tin Woodman rules the Winkies, a position he accepted after Dorothy destroyed the Wicked Witch of the West. Other familiar characters from the previous Oz story return here, such as Glinda the Good. Like Mombi, Glinda doesn't call herself a witch, although that's how she was introduced in the first Oz book. Instead, Glinda has become a sorceress, and that's what she'll be from now on. The Queen of the Field Mice also comes back to offer valuable assistance to Tip and his friends. Other returning characters—the Soldier with the Green Whiskers, the Guardian of the Gate, and the Emerald City maid with green hair—play small but important parts too.

You can be sure though that this Oz story is no rehash of the first. For instance, there are plenty of new magical items. Instead of Silver Shoes and Golden Cap, you'll see the incredible Powder of Life as well as Dr. Nikidik's problematic Wishing Pills at work. New characters fill the panels almost to bursting. Meet fragile, innocent Jack Pumpkinhead and a Sawhorse made all of wood. Then there are the pompous, human-sized insect named Prof. H. M. Woggle-bug, T. E.; a flying contraption known as the Gump; and General Jinjur, leader of the Army of Revolt.

Jinjur's rather absurd female army seems to be author L. Frank Baum's attempt to poke gentle fun at the women's rights movement of his day. Today the idea of women as soldiers is no longer unusual. In fact, these days the author's portrayal of women soldiers as silly airheads could seem offensive if it weren't for three things. First, the other all-female army of the story, the one led by Glinda the Good, is capable, formidable, and never played for laughs. Second, L. Frank Baum was the son-in-law of prominent suffragist and women's rights leader Matilda Joslyn Gage, with whom he enjoyed a close relationship. All evidence suggests that Baum was familiar with and sympathetic to Matilda Gage's views. Gage was even a major early influence on Baum's writings when she strongly encouraged him to write down his stories for children. Because of this, Gage's current biographer has gone so far as to dub Gage the "mother of Oz." And third, the many strong females in Baum's fantasy stories, such as Dorothy Gale, Glinda the Good, and—well, I won't go farther because I don't want to spoil any surprises.

When L. Frank Baum wrote *The Wonderful Wizard of Oz*, he never intended to write a sequel to that book, much less create a series that would be continued for decades after he was gone. So why did *The Marvelous Land of Oz* come into existence?

Baum loved the stage. In fact, he'd been a successful actor, director, and playwright long before *The Wonderful Wizard of Oz* was published. When that book became a bestseller, it was only natural for Baum to adapt his popular story for the stage.

The resulting musical extravaganza of *The Wizard of Oz* was the runaway hit of New York's Broadway in 1903. It made stars of the comedy team that played the Scarecrow and Tin Woodman. It made L. Frank Baum a wealthy man. And it made Oz a household word. Baum hoped to recreate this amazing success, so he sat down to write another Oz book and turn it into a musical extravaganza, too. *The Marvelous Land of Oz* was published in 1904. Baum made sure that his story prominently featured the star characters of the *Wizard* stage musical, the Scarecrow and Tin Woodman, and dedicated the book to the actors who played those characters, Fred Stone and David Montgomery. The endpaper illustration of the book even featured a photograph of the two actors in their Oz costumes.

The stage version of *The Wizard of Oz* contained many features that couldn't be found in the original Oz book. Some of those features made it into *The Marvelous Land of Oz*. For instance, we learn the Tin Woodman's real name, Nick Chopper. In the stage version of *Wizard*, Nick is short for Niccolo—in order to rhyme with piccolo, an instrument the character often played. *The Marvelous Land of Oz* also reveals that the Emerald City was once ruled by a king named Pastoria, a major character in the stage musical who was trying to recover his throne from the Wizard of Oz.

In his attempt to duplicate the riches and popularity brought by *The Wizard of Oz* musical extravaganza, Baum turned *The Marvelous Land of Oz* into a musical extravaganza called *The Woggle-Bug*. Unfortunately for Baum, *The Woggle-Bug* flopped in Chicago and never reached Broadway.

I'll let you in on a secret, though. If you compare this comics version of *The Marvelous Land of Oz* to L. Frank Baum's original book, you might notice some differences, especially in speeches by Mombi and General Jinjur's Army of Revolt. Where did these differences come from? Did I just make them up because I thought L. Frank Baum had fallen down on the job? No. Those differences were written by L. Frank Baum himself—in his script for *The Woggle-Bug*, his stage version of this story. I simply inserted bits of Baum's script into this version wherever I saw that they would enhance the story.

But enough explanation. Get ready—get set—to experience a second journey through *The Marvelous Land of Oz* as seen through the generous eyes of artist Skottie Young and colorist Jean-Francois Beaulieu. Let's go!

Eric Shanower
San Diego, July 2010

Folklore, legends, myths and fairy tales have followed childhood through the ages, for every heal
youngster has a wholesome and instinctive love for stories fantastic, marvelous and manifestly unreal

The story of "The Wonderful Wizard of Oz" was written solely to please children of today. It aspires
being a modernized fairy tale, in which the wonderment and joy are retained and the heartaches a
nightmares are left out.

L. FRANK BAUM, CHICAGO, APRIL 19

THE MARVELOUS LAND OF OZ

ERIC SHANOWER
WRITER

SKOTTIE YOUNG
ARTIST

JEAN-FRANCOIS BEAULIEU
COLORIST

JEFF ECKLEBERRY
LETTERER

ANTHONY DIAL
PRODUCTION

MICHAEL HORWITZ
ASSISTANT EDITOR

NATHAN COSBY
EDITOR

JOE QUESADA
EDITOR IN CHIEF

DAN BUCKLEY
PUBLISHER

ALAN FINE
EXECUTIVE PRODUCER

ADAPTED FROM
THE BOOK BY
L. FRANK BAUM

HA HA HA!

IN THE COUNTRY OF THE GILLIKINS, WHICH IS AT THE NORTH OF THE LAND OF OZ, LIVED A YOUTH CALLED TIP.

OLD MOMBI OFTEN DECLARED THAT HIS WHOLE NAME WAS TIPPETARIUS. BUT NO ONE WAS EXPECTED TO SAY SUCH A LONG WORD WHEN "TIP" WOULD DO JUST AS WELL.

THE BOY REMEMBERED NOTHING OF HIS PARENTS, FOR HE HAD BEEN BROUGHT WHEN QUITE YOUNG TO BE REARED BY THE OLD WOMAN KNOWN AS MOMBI.

MOMBI'S REPUTATION WAS NONE OF THE BEST.

THE GILLIKIN PEOPLE HAD REASON TO SUSPECT MOMBI OF INDULGING IN MAGICAL ARTS, AND THEY HESITATED TO ASSOCIATE WITH HER.

HERE'S WOOD TO BOIL YOUR POT.

MOMBI WAS NOT EXACTLY A WITCH. THE GOOD WITCH WHO RULED THAT PART OF THE LAND OF OZ HAD FORBIDDEN ANY OTHER WITCH TO EXIST IN HER DOMINIONS.

WHAT TOOK YOU SO LONG?

SO MOMBI REALIZED IT WAS UNLAWFUL TO BE MORE THAN A SORCERESS, OR AT MOST A WIZARDESS.

BUT MOMBI'S WEIRD POWERS OFTEN FRIGHTENED HER NEIGHBORS.

CLIMBING TREES -- OR CHASING RABBITS --

-- OR FISHING AGAIN!

TIP FRANKLY HATED HER.

I'LL GO MILK THE COW.

INDEED, HE SOMETIMES SHOWED LESS RESPECT FOR THE OLD WOMAN THAN HE SHOULD HAVE, CONSIDERING SHE WAS HIS GUARDIAN.

I DON'T CARE -- I CAN'T WORK ALL THE TIME. THAT WOULD BE BAD FOR ME.

ONE DAY MOMBI WENT TO THE VILLAGE -- TO BUY GROCERIES, SHE SAID -- A JOURNEY OF AT LEAST TWO DAYS.

I HAVE A NOTION TO GIVE THE OLD WOMAN A FRIGHT.

HERE'S A FINE, BIG PUMPKIN.

HA! WHAT A JOLLY EXPRESSION!

I'LL MAKE THE FORM OF A MAN TO WEAR THIS PUMPKIN HEAD, AND STAND IT IN A PLACE WHERE OLD MOMBI WILL MEET IT FACE TO FACE.

SHE'LL SQUEAL LOUDER THAN THE BROWN PIG DOES WHEN I PULL HER TAIL!

SHE'LL SHIVER WITH FRIGHT WORSE THAN I DID LAST YEAR WHEN I HAD A FEVER!

TIP JOINTED LIMBS AND FASTENED THEM TO THE BODY. HE CAREFULLY ROUNDED ALL THE EDGES AND SMOOTHED THE ROUGH PLACES.

IT'S REMARKABLY TALL. BUT THAT'S GOOD!

TOMORROW I'LL MAKE THE NECK IN ORDER TO FASTEN THE PUMPKIN-HEAD TO THE BODY.

BUT IT WOULD BE MUCH MORE LIFELIKE IF IT WERE PROPERLY DRESSED.

NEXT MORNING.

NOW, THAT OUGHT TO FRIGHTEN SEVERAL SCREECHES OUT OF OLD MOMBI!

TIP RANSACKED THE GREAT CHEST IN WHICH MOMBI KEPT ALL HER KEEPSAKES AND TREASURES. AT THE VERY BOTTOM HE DISCOVERED SOME CLOTHES.

THEY DON'T FIT VERY WELL...

HA! THAT IS REALLY A VERY FINE MAN!

SO GOOD A MAN AS THIS MUST SURELY HAVE A NAME!

I BELIEVE I WILL NAME THE FELLOW *JACK PUMPKIN-HEAD!*

TIP DECIDED THAT THE BEST PLACE TO LOCATE JACK WOULD BE AT THE BEND IN THE ROAD, A LITTLE WAY FROM THE HOUSE.

HE'S *HEAVY* -- AND RATHER AWKWARD TO HANDLE --

UH!

FLUMP

THIS IS HARDER WORK THAN I EVER HAD IN THE FIELD OR FOREST!

AT LAST--

JACK'S ALL RIGHT, AND WORKS FINE -- OH! HIS ARM HAS FALLEN OFF.

THERE IT IS!

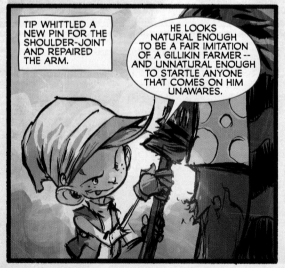

TIP WHITTLED A NEW PIN FOR THE SHOULDER-JOINT AND REPAIRED THE ARM.

HE LOOKS NATURAL ENOUGH TO BE A FAIR IMITATION OF A GILLIKIN FARMER -- AND UNNATURAL ENOUGH TO STARTLE ANYONE THAT COMES ON HIM UNAWARES.

IT'S TOO EARLY TO EXPECT MOMBI. I'LL GO DOWN TO THE VALLEY TO GATHER NUTS.

HOWEVER, MOMBI RETURNED EARLIER THAN USUAL.

I NEED TO GET HOME AS FAST AS I CAN -- IN ORDER TO TEST THE NEW SORCERIES I TRADED FOR WITH THAT CROOKED WIZARD FROM THE MOUNTAINS...

...*THREE* NEW RECIPES, *FOUR* MAGICAL POWDERS, AND A SELECTION OF HERBS OF *WONDERFUL* POWER AND POTENCY!

GOOD EVENING, SIR.

HEH! THAT RASCALLY BOY HAS BEEN PLAYING TRICKS AGAIN! VERY GOOD! VE-E-E-E-RY GOOD!

I'LL BEAT HIM BLACK-AND-BLUE FOR TRYING TO SCARE ME! AND I'LL START WITH --

WAIT, HERE IS A GOOD CHAN... TO TRY MY NE... POWDER!

AND THEN I CAN TELL WHETHER THE CROOKED WIZARD HAS FAIRLY TRADED SECRETS...OR WHETHER HE HAS FOOLED ME AS WICKEDLY AS I FOOLED HIM.

SHE'S BACK ALREADY! AND SHE'S NOT THE LEAST BIT FRIGHTENED.

BUT WHAT IS SHE GOING TO DO?

AH -- HERE IT IS!

THE STINGY WIZARD DIDN'T GIVE ME MUCH OF IT, BUT I GUESS THERE'S ENOUGH FOR TWO OR THREE DOSES.

NOW LET US SEE IF IT IS POTENT.

WEAUGH!

TEAUGH!

PEAUGH!

DON'T YELL LIKE THAT! DO YOU THINK I'M DEAF?

HE LIVES! HE LIVES! HE LIVES!

HA HA HA HA HA!

YOU NAUGHTY, SNEAKING, WICKED BOY! I'LL TEACH YOU TO SPY OUT MY SECRETS AND TO MAKE FUN OF ME!

HA HA HA..

I WASN'T MAKING FUN OF YOU! I WAS LAUGHING AT OLD PUMPKINHEAD! *LOOK* AT HIM!

I HOPE YOU ARE NOT REFLECTING ON MY PERSONAL APPEARANCE.

HA HA HA HA!

WHAT ARE YOU GOING TO DO WITH HIM, NOW THAT HE'S ALIVE?

I MUST THINK IT OVER.

WHAT DO YOU KNOW?

WELL, THAT IS HARD TO TELL -- FOR ALTHOUGH I FEEL THAT I KNOW A TREMENDOUS LOT, I AM NOT YET AWARE HOW MUCH THERE IS IN THE WORLD TO FIND OUT ABOUT.

IT WILL TAKE ME A LITTLE TIME TO DISCOVER WHETHER I AM VERY WISE OR VERY FOOLISH.

TO BE SURE. BUT WE MUST GET HOME AT ONCE, FOR IT IS GROWING DARK.

HELP THE PUMPKINHEAD TO WALK.

NEVER MIND ME. I CAN WALK AS WELL AS YOU CAN. HAVEN'T I GOT LEGS AND FEET, AND AREN'T THEY JOINTED?

ARE THEY?

OF COURSE THEY ARE. I MADE 'EM MYSELF.

MOMBI LED THE PUMPKIN MAN TO THE STABLE AND SHUT HIM UP IN AN EMPTY STALL.

IN THE HOUSE.

LIGHT A CANDLE, THEN BUILD A FIRE IN THE HEARTH.

THE FIRE'S GOING. MAY I HAVE A SHARE OF THE BREAD AND CHEESE?

NO.

I'M HUNGRY!

YOU WON'T BE HUNGRY LONG.

TIP REMEMBERED HE HAD NUTS IN HIS POCKET, SO HE CRACKED AND ATE THEM.

WHAT IS THAT FOR?

FOR YOU.

HAVE I GOT TO DRINK THAT STUFF?

YES.

WHAT'LL IT DO TO ME?

IF IT'S PROPERLY MADE, IT WILL CHANGE OR TRANSFORM YOU INTO A MARBLE STATUE.

UHH... I DON'T WANT TO BE A MARBLE STATUE.

THAT DOESN'T MATTER. I WANT YOU TO BE ONE.

WHAT USE'LL I BE THEN? THERE WON'T BE ANYONE TO WORK FOR YOU.

WHY DON'T YOU CHANGE ME INTO A GOAT -- OR A CHICKEN?

YOU CAN'T DO ANYTHING WITH A MARBLE STATUE.

I'LL MAKE THE PUMPKINHEAD WORK FOR ME.

I'M GOING TO PLANT A FLOWER GARDEN NEXT SPRING, AND I'LL PUT YOU IN THE MIDDLE OF IT FOR AN ORNAMENT.

I WONDER WHY I HAVEN'T THOUGHT OF THAT BEFORE. YOU'VE BEEN A BOTHER TO ME FOR YEARS.

PERHAPS IT WON'T WORK.

OH, I THINK IT WILL. I SELDOM MAKE A MISTAKE.

YOU CANNOT DRINK IT UNTIL IT HAS BECOME QUITE COLD. WE MUST BOTH GO TO BED NOW.

AT DAYBREAK I WILL CALL YOU AND COMPLETE YOUR TRANSFORMATION INTO A MARBLE STATUE.

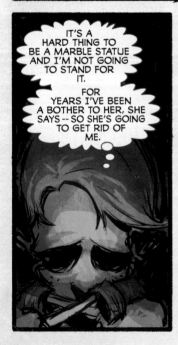

IT'S A HARD THING TO BE A MARBLE STATUE AND I'M NOT GOING TO STAND FOR IT.

FOR YEARS I'VE BEEN A BOTHER TO HER, SHE SAYS -- SO SHE'S GOING TO GET RID OF ME.

WELL, THERE'S AN EASIER WAY THAN TO BECOME A STATUE.

I'LL *RUN AWAY*, THAT'S WHAT I'LL DO.

NO USE STARTING ON A JOURNEY WITHOUT FOOD.

HERE'S CHEESE AND --

I MAY AS WELL TAKE *THIS* WITH ME -- OR MOMBI'LL BE USING IT TO MAKE MORE MISCHIEF WITH.

I'LL BE GLAD TO GET AWAY, FOR I NEVER DID LIKE THAT OLD WOMAN. I WONDER HOW I EVER CAME TO LIVE WITH HER.

JACK PUMPKINHEAD BELONGS TO ME, FOR I MADE HIM -- EVEN IF THE OLD WITCH DID BRING HIM TO LIFE.

COME ON!

WHERE TO?

YOU'LL KNOW AS SOON AS I DO. ALL WE'VE GOT TO DO IS TRAMP.

VERY WELL.

OH!

SH!

THE JOINTS OF MY LEGS TURN BACKWARD AS WELL AS FRONTWISE. I'LL TAKE MORE PAINS TO STEP CAREFULLY.

I SEE WE CAN'T GO VERY FAST.

THEY TURNED FIRST INTO ONE PATH, AND THEN INTO ANOTHER, SO THAT IT WOULD PROVE DIFFICULT TO GUESS WHICH WAY THEY HAD GONE.

BUT IF WE WALK STEADILY WITHOUT STOPPING AN INSTANT, WE SHALL TRAVEL A GREAT DISTANCE BY THE TIME THE SUN PEEPS OVER THE HILLS.

AT SUNRISE, FAIRLY SATISFIED THAT HE HAD ESCAPED PURSUIT FROM THE OLD WITCH -- FOR A TIME, AT LEAST -- TIP STOPPED BY THE ROADSIDE.

LET'S HAVE SOME BREAKFAST.

I DON'T SEEM TO BE MADE THE SAME WAY YOU ARE.

I KNOW YOU AREN'T, FOR I MADE YOU.

OH! DID YOU?

CERTAINLY. AND PUT YOU TOGETHER. AND CARVED YOUR EYES AND NOSE AND MOUTH. AND DRESSED YOU.

IT STRIKES ME YOU MADE A VERY GOOD JOB OF IT.

JUST SO-SO. IF I'D KNOWN WE WERE GOING TO TRAVEL TOGETHER I MIGHT HAVE BEEN A LITTLE MORE PARTICULAR.

THEN, YOU MUST BE MY CREATOR -- MY PARENT -- MY *FATHER!*

OR YOUR INVENTOR. HA! YES, MY SON, I REALLY BELIEVE I AM!

THEN I OWE YOU OBEDIENCE. AND YOU OWE ME -- SUPPORT.

THAT'S IT, EXACTLY. SO LET'S BE OFF.

WHERE ARE WE GOING?

I BELIEVE WE'RE HEADED SOUTH. THAT'LL BRING US, SOONER OR LATER, TO THE EMERALD CITY.

WHAT CITY IS THAT?

IT'S THE CENTER OF THE LAND OF OZ. I'VE NEVER BEEN THERE, BUT IT WAS BUILT BY A WONDERFUL WIZARD NAMED OZ.

EVERYTHING THERE IS GREEN -- JUST AS EVERYTHING IN THIS COUNTRY OF THE GILLIKINS IS PURPLE.

IS EVERYTHING HERE PURPLE?

OF COURSE. CAN'T YOU SEE?

I BELIEVE I MUST BE COLOR-BLIND.

WELL, THE GRASS IS PURPLE, AND THE TREES ARE PURPLE, AND THE HOUSES AND FENCES ARE PURPLE. EVEN THE MUD IN THE ROAD IS PURPLE.

BUT IN THE EMERALD CITY EVERYTHING IS GREEN THAT IS PURPLE HERE.

IN THE COUNTRY OF THE MUNCHKINS, AT THE EAST, EVERY-THING IS BLUE. IN THE SOUTH COUNTRY OF THE QUADLINGS, EVERY-THING IS RED. AND IN THE WEST, WHERE THE TIN WOODMAN RULES THE WINKIES, EVERYTHING IS YELLOW.

OH! DID YOU SAY A TIN WOODMAN RULES THE WINKIES?

YES, HE HELPED DESTROY THE WICKED WITCH OF THE WEST, AND THE WINKIES INVITED HIM TO BE THEIR RULER -- JUST AS THE PEOPLE OF THE EMERALD CITY INVITED THE SCARE-CROW TO RULE THEM.

DEAR ME! I'M GETTING CONFUSED WITH ALL THIS HISTORY. WHO IS THE SCARECROW?

I TOLD YOU. HE RULES THE EMERALD CITY.

I THOUGHT YOU SAID IT WAS RULED BY A WIZARD.

PAY ATTENTION, AND I'LL EXPLAIN.

DOROTHY WAS A GIRL THAT CAME HERE FROM KANSAS, A PLACE IN THE BIG, OUTSIDE WORLD. DOROTHY WENT TO THE EMERALD CITY TO ASK THE WIZARD TO SEND HER BACK, AND THE SCARECROW AND TIN WOODMAN WENT WITH HER.

BUT THE WIZARD COULDN'T SEND HER BACK. AND THEY GOT ANGRY AT THE WIZARD, SO HE MADE A BIG BALLOON AND ESCAPED, AND NO ONE HAS SEEN HIM SINCE.

THEN GLINDA THE GOOD, WHO RULES THE QUADLINGS, SENT DOROTHY HOME AGAIN, AND THE PEOPLE OF THE EMERALD CITY MADE THE SCARECROW THEIR KING.

DO YOU SEE?

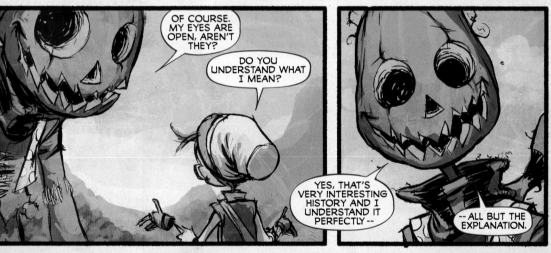

OF COURSE. MY EYES ARE OPEN, AREN'T THEY?

DO YOU UNDERSTAND WHAT I MEAN?

YES, THAT'S VERY INTERESTING HISTORY AND I UNDERSTAND IT PERFECTLY --

-- ALL BUT THE EXPLANATION.

I'M GLAD YOU DO.

ARE WE GOING TO SEE THIS SCARECROW KING?

WE MAY AS WELL -- UNLESS YOU HAVE SOMETHING BETTER TO DO.

OH, NO, DEAR FATHER. I'M QUITE WILLING TO GO WHEREVER YOU PLEASE.

THEY JOURNEYED ON.

ARE YOU TIRED?

OF COURSE NOT. BUT IT'S QUITE CERTAIN I SHALL WEAR OUT MY WOODEN JOINTS IF I KEEP ON WALKING.

WHY DON'T YOU SIT DOWN?

WON'T IT STRAIN MY JOINTS?

OF COURSE NOT. IT'LL REST THEM.

CLATTER

IS YOUR HEAD CRACKED?

GUESS YOU BETTER REMAIN STANDING. IT SEEMS THE SAFEST WAY.

VERY WELL, DEAR FATHER. JUST AS YOU SAY.

WHAT IS THAT THING YOU ARE SITTING ON?

OH, THIS IS A HORSE.

WHAT IS A HORSE?

A HORSE? THERE ARE *TWO* KINDS OF HORSES. ONE KIND IS ALIVE, AND HAS FOUR LEGS AND A HEAD AND TAIL. AND PEOPLE RIDE UPON ITS BACK.

I UNDERSTAND. THAT'S THE KIND OF HORSE YOU'RE NOW SITTING ON.

NO, IT ISN'T.

WHY NOT? THAT ONE HAS FOUR LEGS, AND A HEAD, AND A TAIL.

THIS THING RESEMBLES A REAL HORSE MORE THAN I SUSPECTED. BUT A REAL HORSE IS ALIVE, AND TROTS AND PRANCES AND EATS OATS.

THIS ISN'T A REAL HORSE, ANY MORE THAN YOU'RE A REAL MAN. IT WAS MADE TO SAW LOGS ON. THAT'S WHY THEY CALL IT A SAW-HORSE.

IF IT WERE ALIVE, WOULDN'T IT TROT, AND PRANCE, AND EAT OATS, AND--

IT WOULD TROT AND PRANCE, PERHAPS. BUT IT WOULDN'T EAT OATS. AND IT CAN'T EVER BE ALIVE, BECAUSE IT IS MADE OF WOOD.

SO AM I. ALL BUT THE PUMPKIN.

WHY, SO YOU ARE! AND THE MAGIC POWDER THAT BROUGHT YOU TO LIFE IS HERE IN MY POCKET!

I WONDER IF IT WOULD BRING THE SAW-HORSE TO LIFE.

IF IT WOULD, I COULD RIDE ON ITS BACK, AND THAT WOULD SAVE MY JOINTS FROM WEARING OUT.

I'LL TRY IT!

IT DID THE JOB FOR ME, ALL RIGHT.

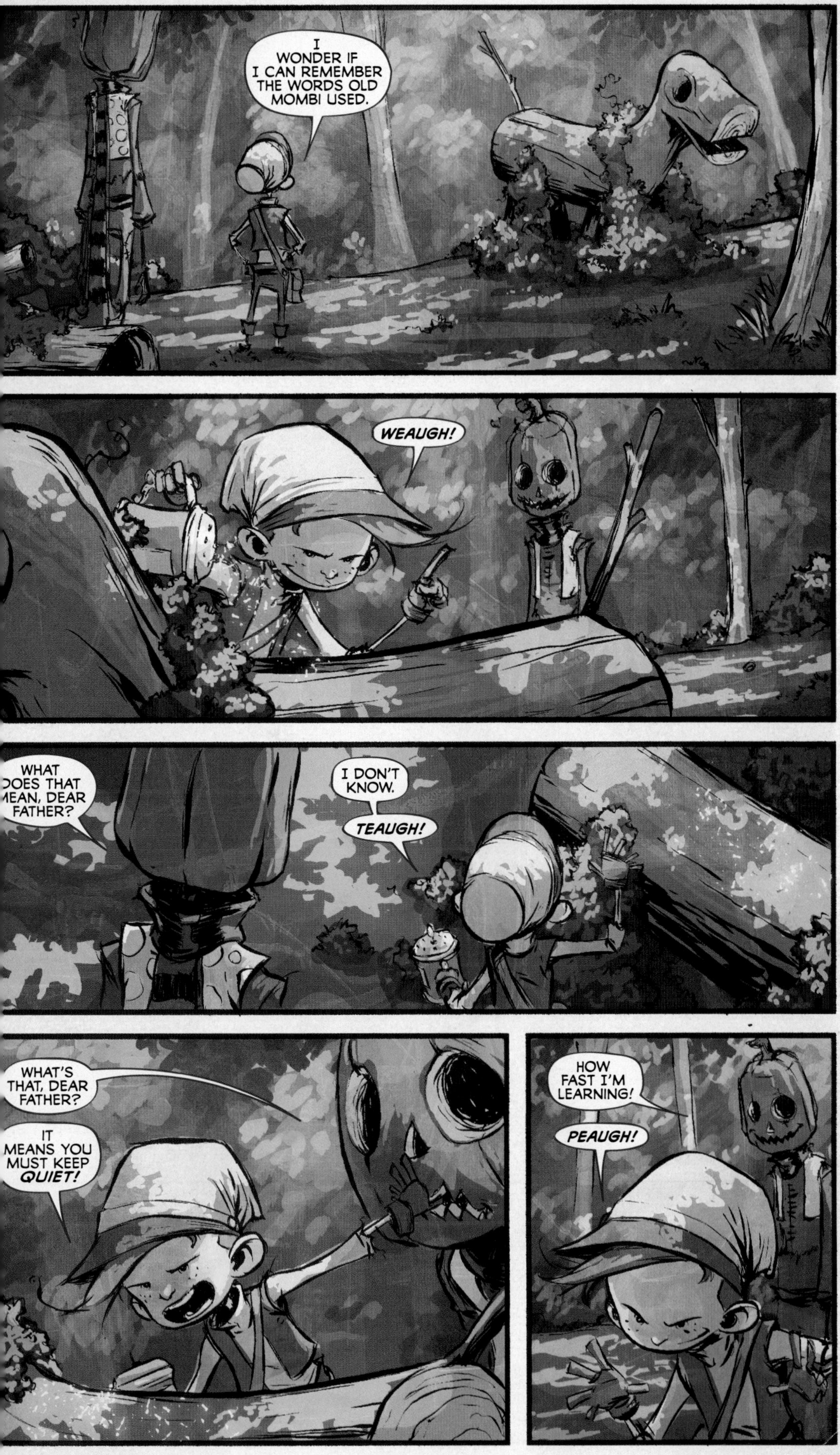
I WONDER IF I CAN REMEMBER THE WORDS OLD MOMBI USED.
WEAUGH!
WHAT DOES THAT MEAN, DEAR FATHER?
I DON'T KNOW.
TEAUGH!
WHAT'S THAT, DEAR FATHER?
IT MEANS YOU MUST KEEP *QUIET!*
HOW FAST I'M LEARNING!
PEAUGH!

YOU'RE A VERY CLEVER SORCERER, DEAR FATHER.

WHOA! WHOA, THERE!

BUMP!

WHOA -- OW!

WHOA! WHOA!

I DON'T BELIEVE THE ANIMAL CAN HEAR YOU.

I SHOUT LOUD ENOUGH, DON'T I?

YES, BUT THE THING HAS NO EARS.

GOOD BOY! GOOD BOY!

I MUST FIND A HALTER FOR HIM.

*T*IP SEARCHED HIS POCKETS AND FOUND A STRONG CORD, WHICH HE TIED AROUND THE SAWHORSE'S NECK.

HE'S STRONGER THAN I THOUGHT... AND OBSTINATE, TOO.

WHY DON'T YOU MAKE HIM SOME EARS? THEN YOU CAN TELL HIM WHAT TO DO.

THAT'S A SPLENDID IDEA, JACK! HOW DID YOU HAPPEN TO THINK OF IT?

I DIDN'T THINK OF IT -- I DIDN'T NEED TO, FOR IT'S THE SIMPLEST AND EASIEST THING TO DO.

I MUSTN'T MAKE THE EARS TOO BIG, OR OUR HORSE WOULD BECOME A DONKEY.

A HORSE HAS BIGGER EARS THAN A MAN, AND A DONKEY HAS BIGGER EARS THAN A HORSE.

IF *MY* EARS WERE LONGER, WOULD *I* BE A HORSE?

YOU'LL NEVER BE ANYTHING BUT A PUMPKINHEAD, NO MATTER HOW BIG YOUR EARS ARE.

OH, I THINK I UNDERSTAND -- EVEN IF I DO HAVE TO DO MY THINKING WITH PUMPKIN SEEDS.

THERE'S NO HARM IN *THINKING* YOU UNDERSTAND -- IT' A WONDER YOU C/ THINK AT ALL. I C/ HEAR YOUR SEED RATTLE WHEN YOU TRY TO BE SMART.

I GUESS THESE EARS ARE READY NOW. WILL YOU HOLD THE HORSE WHILE I STICK THEM ON?

CERTAINLY, IF YOU'LL HELP ME UP.

*T*IP BORED TWO HOLES AND INSERTED THE EARS.

THEY MAKE HIM LOOK VERY HANDSOME.

THESE WORDS, BEING THE FIRST SOUNDS THE SAWHORSE HAD EVER HEARD, STARTLED HIM.

WHOA!

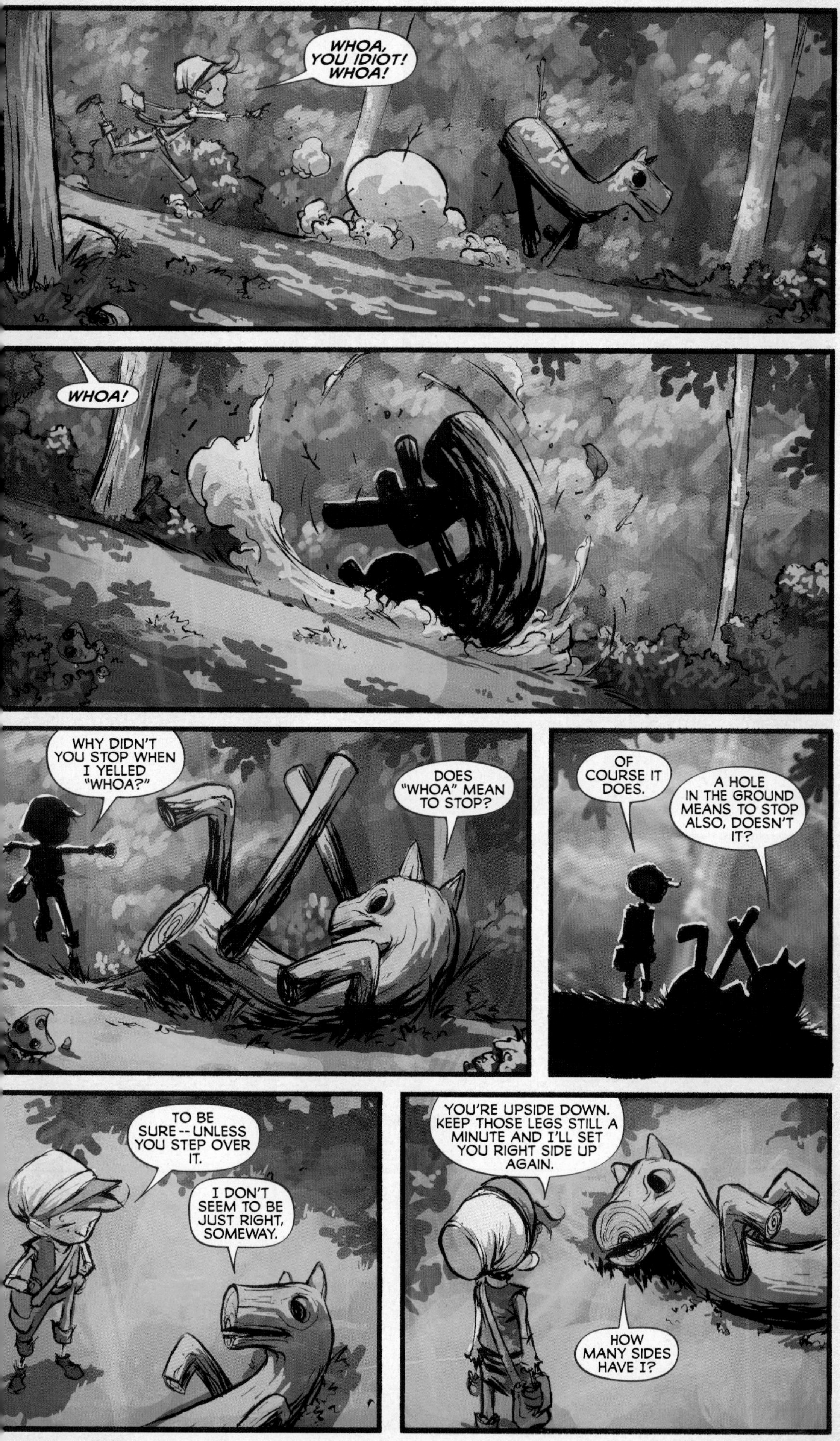

WHOA, YOU IDIOT! WHOA!
WHOA!
WHY DIDN'T YOU STOP WHEN I YELLED "WHOA?"
DOES "WHOA" MEAN TO STOP?
OF COURSE IT DOES.
A HOLE IN THE GROUND MEANS TO STOP ALSO, DOESN'T IT?
TO BE SURE--UNLESS YOU STEP OVER IT.
I DON'T SEEM TO BE JUST RIGHT, SOMEWAY.
YOU'RE UPSIDE DOWN. KEEP THOSE LEGS STILL A MINUTE AND I'LL SET YOU RIGHT SIDE UP AGAIN.
HOW MANY SIDES HAVE I?

SEVERAL.

AH! I SEEM ALL RIGHT NOW.

ONE OF YOUR EARS IS BROKEN -- I'LL HAVE TO MAKE A NEW ONE.

NOW, PAY ATTENTION. *"WHOA!"* MEANS TO STOP.

"GET-UP!" MEANS TO WALK FORWARD.

"TROT!" MEANS TO GO AS FAST AS YOU CAN. UNDERSTAND?

I BELIEVE I DO.

*T*IP WHITTLED A NEW EAR FOR THE SAWHORSE.

I'M TIP. I'VE BROUGHT YOU TO LIFE, BUT IT WON'T HURT YOU ANY, IF YOU MIND ME AND DO AS I TELL YOU.

HOLD ON TIGHT, JACK, OR YOU MAY FALL OFF AND CRACK YOUR PUMPKIN HEAD.

THAT WOULD BE HORRIBLE! WHA SHALL I HOLD ON TO?

WE'RE ALL GOING TO THE EMERALD CITY TO SEE HIS MAJESTY, THE SCARECROW. JACK PUMPKINHEAD IS GOING TO RIDE ON YOUR BACK, SO HE WON'T WEAR OUT HIS JOINTS.

ANYTHING THAT SUITS YOU SUITS ME.

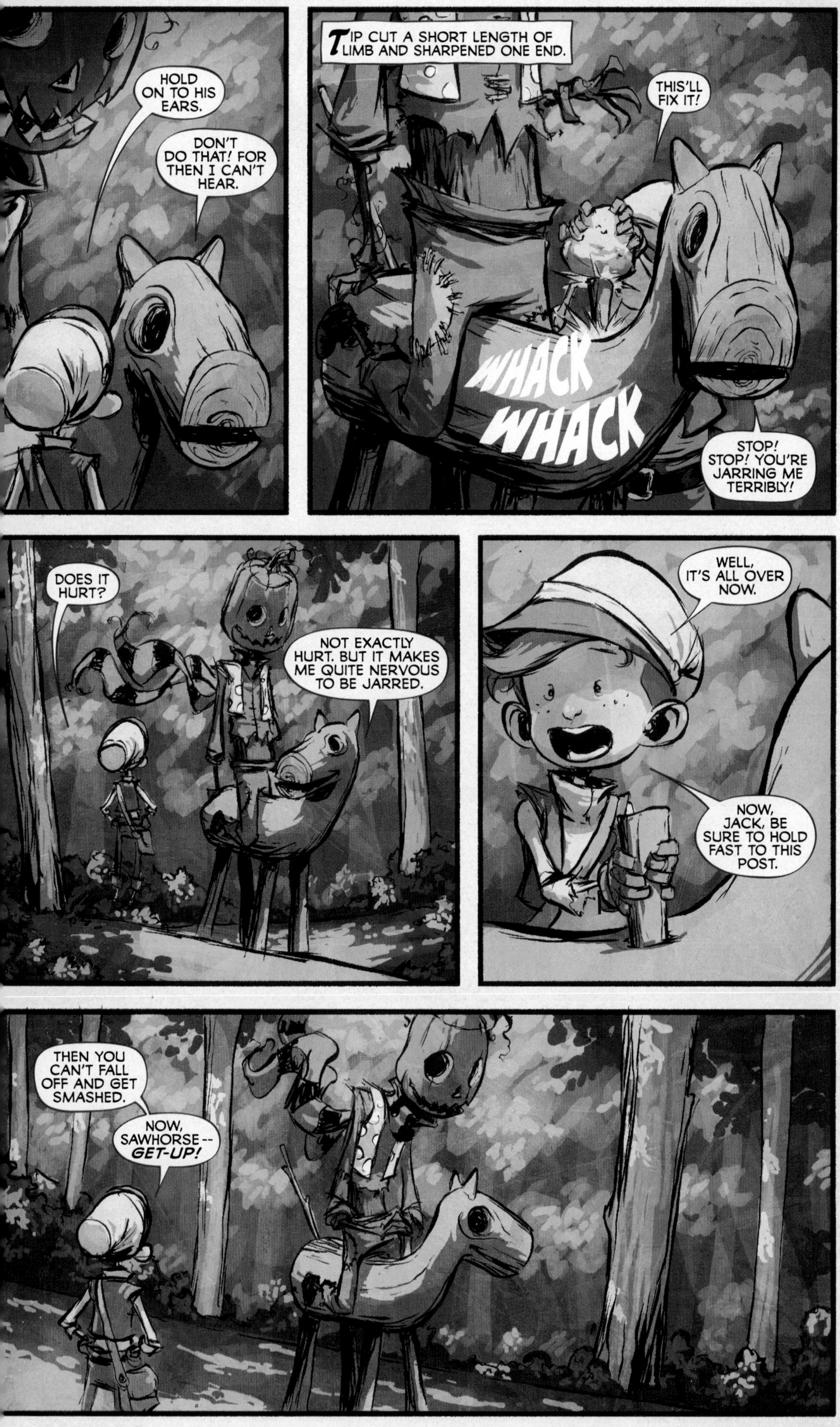
HOLD ON TO HIS EARS.
DON'T DO THAT! FOR THEN I CAN'T HEAR.
TIP CUT A SHORT LENGTH OF LIMB AND SHARPENED ONE END.
THIS'LL FIX IT!
WHACK
WHACK
STOP! STOP! YOU'RE JARRING ME TERRIBLY!
DOES IT HURT?
NOT EXACTLY HURT. BUT IT MAKES ME QUITE NERVOUS TO BE JARRED.
WELL, IT'S ALL OVER NOW.
NOW, JACK, BE SURE TO HOLD FAST TO THIS POST.
THEN YOU CAN'T FALL OFF AND GET SMASHED.
NOW, SAWHORSE-- *GET-UP!*

WHAT DOES THAT SOUND MEAN?

I'M JUST WHISTLING, AND THAT ONLY MEANS I'M PRETTY WELL SATISFIED.

I'D WHISTLE MYSELF, IF I COULD PUSH MY LIPS TOGETHER. I FEAR, DEAR FATHER, THAT IN SOME RESPECTS I AM SADLY LACKING.

*T*HEY CAMPED FOR THE NIGHT BY THE ROADSIDE. TIP LEFT THE SAW-HORSE TO STAND WATCH.

AT DAYBREAK TIP BATHED IN A LITTLE BROOK, THEN ATE A PORTION OF HIS BREAD AND CHEESE, AND THE JOURNEY WAS RESUMED.

THE NARROW PATH THEY WERE FOLLOWING TURNED INTO A BROAD ROADWAY PAVED WITH YELLOW BRICK.

NINE MILES IS QUITE A DISTANCE, BUT WE OUGHT TO REACH THE EMERALD CITY BY NOON IF NO ACCIDENTS HAPPEN.

9 miles to the Emerald City

THEY TRAVELED TWO MILES--

FERRYMAN! WILL YOU ROW US TO THE OTHER SIDE?

YES, IF YOU HAVE MONEY!

BUT I HAVE NO MONEY.

THEN I'LL NOT BREAK MY BACK ROWING YOU OVER!

WHAT A NICE MAN!

BUT HOW CAN I CROSS THE RIVER IF YOU DON'T TAKE ME?

HAW! THAT WOODEN HORSE WILL FLOAT AND YOU CAN RIDE HIM ACROSS. AS FOR THAT PUMPKIN-HEADED LOON, LET HIM SINK OR SWIM -- IT WON'T MATTER GREATLY WHICH.

TIP THOUGHT THE EXPERIMENT WAS WORTH MAKING.

BE SURE TO KEEP YOUR PUMPKIN-HEAD ABOVE THE WATER, JACK.

DON'T WORRY ABOUT ME -- I'M SURE I OUGHT TO FLOAT BEAUTIFULLY.

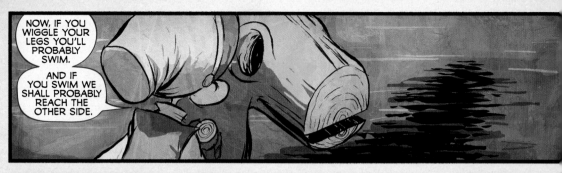

NOW, IF YOU WIGGLE YOUR LEGS YOU'LL PROBABLY SWIM.

AND IF YOU SWIM WE SHALL PROBABLY REACH THE OTHER SIDE.

HAW HAW HAW!

ANYHOW, WE ARE SAFELY ACROSS, IN SPITE OF THE FERRY-MAN.

I DIDN'T MIND SWIMMING AT ALL.

NOR DID I.

IF YOU RIDE FAST, THE WIND WILL HELP TO DRY YOUR CLOTHING. I'LL HOLD ON TO THE HORSE'S TAIL AND RUN AFTER YOU.

THEN THE HORSE MUST STEP LIVELY.

I'LL DO MY BEST.

GET-UP!

TIP DECIDED THEY COULD GO FASTER.

TROT!

THE SAWHORSE REMEMBERED THAT THIS WAS THE COMMAND TO GO AS FAST AS HE COULD.

SNAP!

WH -- KOFF! KOFF!

HAKK! KOFF!

BY THE TIME TIP HAD CLEARED HIS THROAT SO HE COULD SAY "WHOA!" THE HORSE WAS OUT OF SIGHT.

SO HE DID THE ONLY SENSIBLE THING HE COULD DO.

IF I WALK ALONG THE ROAD, SOMETIME I'LL OVERTAKE THEM. ALL THE ROADS PAVED WITH YELLOW BRICK END AT THE GATES OF THE EMERALD CITY -- THEY CAN'T GO FURTHER THAN THAT.

NEITHER JACK NOR THE SAWHORSE KNEW TIP WAS LEFT BEHIND.

WHOA!

SHOOOOOFFF

THAT WAS A FAST RIDE, DEAR FATHER!

FATHER?

I AM THE GUARDIAN OF THE GATES OF THE EMERALD CITY. MAY I INQUIRE WHO YOU ARE, AND WHAT IS YOUR BUSINESS?

MY NAME IS JACK PUMPKINHEAD -- BUT AS TO MY BUSINESS, I HAVEN'T THE LEAST IDEA IN THE WORLD WHAT IT IS.

WHAT ARE YOU, A MAN OR A PUMPKIN?

BOTH, IF YOU PLEASE.

AND THIS WOODEN HORSE -- IS IT ALIVE?

OUCH!

I'M SORRY I ASKED THE QUESTION -- BUT THE ANSWER IS MOST CONVINCING! HAVE YOU ANY ERRAND, SIR, IN THE EMERALD CITY?

IT SEEMS TO ME THAT I HAVE, BUT I CAN'T THINK WHAT IT IS. MY FATHER KNOWS ALL ABOUT IT, BUT HE ISN'T HERE.

VERY STRANGE! BUT YOU SEEM HARMLESS. FOLKS DO NOT SMILE SO DELIGHTFULLY WHEN THEY MEAN MISCHIEF.

I CANNOT HELP MY SMILE, FOR IT'S CARVED ON MY FACE WITH A JACKKNIFE.

WELL, COME WITH ME AND I WILL SEE WHAT CAN BE DONE FOR YOU.

*T*HE GUARDIAN PULLED A BELLCORD, AND PRESENTLY --

HERE IS A STRANGE GENTLEMAN WHO DOESN'T KNOW WHY HE HAS COME TO THE EMERALD CITY OR WHAT HE WANTS. WHAT SHALL WE DO WITH HIM?

I MUST TAKE HIM TO HIS MAJESTY, THE SCARECROW.

BUT WHAT WILL HIS MAJESTY DO WITH HIM?

THAT'S HIS MAJESTY'S BUSINESS. I HAVE TROUBLES ENOUGH OF MY OWN.

PUT THE SPECTACLES ON THIS FELLOW AND I'LL TAKE HI[M] TO THE ROYAL PALACE.

HIS HEAD IS SO BIG I SHALL BE OBLIGED TO TIE THE SPECTACLES ON.

BUT WHY DO I NEED SPECTACLES?

IT'S THE FASHION HERE -- THEY'LL KEEP YOU FROM BEING BLINDED BY THE GLITTER OF THE GORGEOUS EMERALD CITY.

OH! TIE THEM ON -- I DON'T WISH TO BE BLINDED.

NOR I!

THE SOLDIER WITH THE GREEN WHISKERS LED THEM THROUGH THE EMERALD CITY.

THE PUMPKINHEAD AND THE SAWHORSE SCARCELY NOTICED THE CROWDS WHO STOOD IN SURPRISE.

KNOWING NOTHING OF WEALTH AND BEAUTY, THEY PAID LITTLE ATTENTION TO THE WONDERFUL SIGHTS.

AT THE ROYAL PALACE JACK DISMOUNTED WITH MUCH DIFFICULTY.

A SERVANT WILL LEAD YOUR SAWHORSE AROUND TO THE REAR WHILE I ESCORT YOU INTO THE PALACE BY THE FRONT ENTRANCE.

JACK WAS LEFT IN A WAITING-ROOM WHILE THE SOLDIER WENT TO ANNOUNCE HIM.

IT SO HAPPENS THAT AT THIS HOUR HIS MAJESTY IS AT LEISURE AND GREATLY BORE FOR WANT OF SOMETHING TO DO, SO HE ORDERS HIS VISITOR TO BE SHOWN AT ONCE INTO HIS THRONE ROOM.

JACK FELT NO FEAR AT MEETING THE RULER OF THIS MAGNIFICENT CITY, BUT HE WAS MORE SURPRISED AT THE STRANGE APPEARANCE OF THIS REMARKABLE KING THAN BY ANY OTHER EXPERIENCE OF HIS BRIEF LIFE.

AT FIRST, HIS MAJESTY THE SCARECROW THOUGHT HIS VISITOR WAS LAUGHING AT HIM AND WAS INCLINED TO RESENT SUCH A LIBERTY.

BUT IT WAS NOT WITHOUT REASON THAT THE SCARECROW HAD ATTAINED THE REPUTATION OF BEING THE WISEST PERSONAGE IN THE LAND OF OZ.

HE SOON SAW THAT JACK'S FEATURES WERE CARVED INTO A SMILE AND THAT HE COULDN'T LOOK GRAVE IF HE WISHED TO.

WHERE ON EARTH DID YOU COME FROM, AND HOW DO YOU HAPPEN TO BE ALIVE?

I BEG YOUR MAJESTY'S PARDON, BUT I DON'T UNDERSTAND YOU.

WHAT DON'T YOU UNDERSTAND?

I DON'T UNDERSTAND YOUR LANGUAGE. YOU SEE, I CAME FROM THE COUNTRY OF THE GILLIKINS, SO I'M A FOREIGNER.

AH -- TO BE SURE! I SUPPOSE YOU SPEAK THE LANGUAGE OF THE PUMPKIN-HEADS.

EXACTLY, YOUR MAJESTY, SO IT WILL BE IMPOSSIBLE FOR US TO UNDERSTAND ONE ANOTHER.

WE MUST HAVE AN INTERPRETER!

WHAT'S AN INTERPRETER?

A PERSON WHO UNDERSTANDS BOTH MY LANGUAGE AND YOUR OWN.

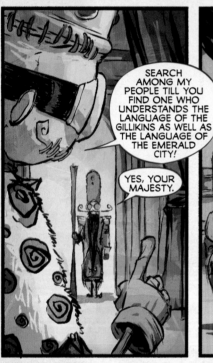

SEARCH AMONG MY PEOPLE TILL YOU FIND ONE WHO UNDERSTANDS THE LANGUAGE OF THE GILLIKINS AS WELL AS THE LANGUAGE OF THE EMERALD CITY!

YES, YOUR MAJESTY.

WON'T YOU TAKE A CHAIR WHILE WE ARE WAITING?

YOUR MAJESTY FORGETS THAT I CANNOT UNDERSTAND YOU. IF YOU WISH ME TO SIT DOWN, YOU MUST MAKE A SIGN FOR ME TO DO SO.

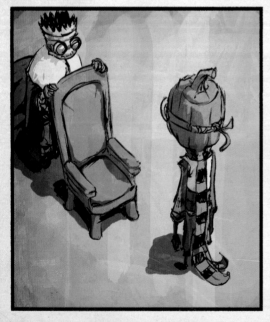

DID YOU UNDERSTAND THAT SIGN?

PERFECTLY.

THERE IS THIS DIFFERENCE BETWEEN US -- *I* WILL BEND BUT NOT BREAK. *YOU* WILL BREAK BUT NOT BEND.

YOUR MAJESTY--

WHY, IT'S JELLIA JAMB! DO YOU UNDERSTAND THE LANGUAGE OF THE GILLIKINS, MY DEAR?

WELL... YES, YOUR MAJESTY, FOR I WAS BORN IN THE NORTH COUNTRY.

THEN YOU CAN BE OUR INTERPRETER AND EXPLAIN TO THIS PUMPKINHEAD ALL THAT I SAY...

VERY SATISFACTORY INDEED.

...AND ALSO EXPLAIN TO ME ALL THAT *HE* SAYS.

IS THIS ARRANGEMENT SATISFACTORY?

JELLIA, ASK HIM -- TO BEGIN WITH -- WHAT BROUGHT HIM TO THE EMERALD CITY.

YOU CERTAINLY ARE A WONDERFUL CREATURE. WHO MADE YOU?

A BOY NAMED TIP.

MY EARS MUST HAVE DECEIVED ME.

WHAT DID HE SAY?

HE SAYS THAT YOUR MAJESTY'S BRAINS SEEM TO HAVE COME LOOSE.

HM. WHAT A FINE THING IT IS TO UNDERSTAND TWO DIFFERENT LANGUAGES.

ASK HIM, MY DEAR, IF HE HAS ANY OBJECTION TO BEING PUT IN JAIL FOR INSULTING THE RULER OF THE EMERALD CITY.

I DIDN'T INSULT YOU!

TUT-TUT! WAIT UNTIL JELLIA TRANSLATES MY SPEECH.

WHAT HAVE WE GOT AN INTERPRETER FOR IF YOU BREAK OUT IN THIS RASH WAY?

ALL RIGHT, I'LL WAIT.

HIS MAJESTY INQUIRES IF YOU ARE HUNGRY.

OH, NOT AT ALL! IT IS IMPOSSIBLE FOR ME TO EAT.

IT'S THE SAME WAY WITH ME.

WHAT DID HE SAY, JELLIA, MY DEAR?

E ASKED IF YOU ERE AWARE THAT NE OF YOUR EYES PAINTED LARGER THAN THE OTHER.

DON'T YOU BELIEVE HER, YOUR MAJESTY!

OH, I DON'T!

JELLIA, ARE YOU QUITE CERTAIN YOU UNDERSTAND BOTH THE LANGUAGES OF THE GILLIKINS AND THE EMERALD CITY?

QUITE CERTAIN, YOUR MAJESTY -- BECAUSE THEY ARE ONE AND THE SAME! DOESN'T YOUR MAJESTY KNOW THAT IN ALL THE LAND OF OZ ONLY ONE LANGUAGE IS SPOKEN?

IT WAS ALL MY FAULT, YOUR MAJESTY. I THOUGHT WE MUST SURELY SPEAK DIFFERENT LANGUAGES, SINCE WE CAME FROM DIFFERENT COUNTRIES.

THIS SHOULD BE A WARNING TO YOU NEVER TO THINK.

IT SEEMS TO ME THAT YOUR MANUFACTURER SPOILED SOME GOOD PIES TO CREATE AN INDIFFERENT MAN.

I ASSURE YOUR MAJESTY THAT I DIDN'T ASK TO BE CREATED.

AH! IT WAS THE SAME IN MY CASE. AND SO, AS WE DIFFER FROM ALL ORDINARY PEOPLE, LET US BECOME FRIENDS.

WITH ALL MY HEART!

WHAT! HAVE YOU A HEART?

NO -- THAT WAS ONLY A FIGURE OF SPEECH.

WELL, YOUR MOST PROMINENT FIGURE SEEMS TO BE A FIGURE OF WOOD, SO I MUST ASK YOU TO RESTRAIN YOUR IMAGINATION WHICH, HAVING NO BRAINS, YOU HAVE NO RIGHT TO EXERCISE.

UHH -- TO BE SURE!

COME, MY NEW FRIEND, I'LL DISMISS JELLIA AND THE SOLDIER, AND WHEN THEY'RE GONE, I'LL TAKE YOU INTO THE COURTYARD TO PLAY A GAME OF QUOITS.

MEANWHILE, TIP WALKED HALF THE DISTANCE TO THE EMERALD CITY WITHOUT STOPPING.

I'M HUNGRY, BUT THE CRACKERS AND CHEESE ARE GONE.

I WONDER WHAT -- OH!

ER... PARDON ME -- IS THERE ENOUGH LUNCH TO --?

THERE! IT'S ME FOR ME TO GO.

CARRY THAT BASKET FOR ME AND HELP YOURSELF TO ITS CONTENTS IF YOU'RE HUNGRY.

THANK YOU VERY MUCH. MAY I ASK YOUR NAME?

I AM GENERAL JINJUR.

WHAT SORT OF A GENERAL?

I COMMAND THE ARMY OF REVOLT IN THIS WAR!

OH! I DIDN'T KNOW THERE WAS A WAR.

YOU WERE NOT SUPPOSED TO KNOW IT -- WE HAVE KEPT IT A SECRET.

AND CONSIDERING THAT OUR ARMY IS COMPOSED ENTIRELY OF GIRLS, IT'S REMARKABLE THAT OUR REVOLT IS NOT YET DISCOVERED.

BUT WHERE'S YOUR ARMY?

ABOUT A MILE FROM HERE. THE FORCES HAVE ASSEMBLED FROM ALL PARTS OF THE LAND OF OZ, AT MY EXPRESS COMMAND.

THE EMERALD CITY HAS BEEN RULED BY MEN LONG ENOUGH!

WITH A GREAT ARMY OF GALLANT MILKMAIDS AND SCULLERY LADIES I'M ABOUT TO MARCH UPON THE EMERALD CITY, CONQUER HIS MAJESTY THE SCARECROW, WREST FROM HIM THE THRONE -- AND RULE THE NATION IN THE EXCLUSIVE INTEREST OF THE FAIR SEX!

MOREOVER, THE CITY GLITTERS WITH BEAUTIFUL GEMS, WHICH MIGHT FAR BETTER BE USED FOR RINGS, BRACELETS, AND NECKLACES.

AND THERE'S ENOUGH MONEY IN THE TREASURY TO BUY EVERY GIRL IN OUR ARMY A DOZEN NEW GOWNS.

BUT WAR IS A TERRIBLE THING. MANY OF YOU WILL BE SLAIN!

OH NO, THIS WAR WILL BE PLEASANT. WHAT MAN WOULD OPPOSE A GIRL, OR DARE TO HARM HER? THERE'S NOT AN UGLY FACE IN MY ENTIRE ARMY.

PERHAPS YOU'RE RIGHT. BUT THE KING'S ARMY WON'T LET THE CITY BE CONQUERED WITHOUT A STRUGGLE.

THE ARMY IS OLD AND FEEBLE. HIS STRENGTH HAS ALL BEEN USED TO GROW WHISKERS, AND HIS WIFE HAS SUCH A TEMPER SHE'S PULLED HALF OF THEM OUT BY THE ROOTS.

WHEN THE WIZARD REIGNED, THE SOLDIER WITH THE GREEN WHISKERS WAS A GOOD ROYAL ARMY, FOR PEOPLE FEARED THE WIZARD.

BUT NO ONE IS AFRAID OF THE SCARECROW, SO HIS ROYAL ARMY DOESN'T COUNT FOR MUCH IN TIME OF WAR.

BEFORE LONG THEY REACHED A CLEARING WHERE FOUR HUNDRED YOUNG WOMEN WERE ASSEMBLED, LAUGHING AND TALKING AS IF THEY HAD GATHERED FOR A PICNIC INSTEAD OF A WAR.

FRIENDS, FELLOW CITIZENS, AND GIRLS!

WE ARE ABOUT TO BEGIN OUR GREAT REVOLT AGAINST THE MEN OF OZ! WE MARCH TO CONQUER THE EMERALD CITY -- TO DETHRONE THE SCARECROW KING --

-- TO ACQUIRE THOUSANDS OF GORGEOUS GEMS --

LIFE'S TOO SHORT TO PAY A DOLLAR DOWN A WEEK FOR POMPADOUR CORONETS!

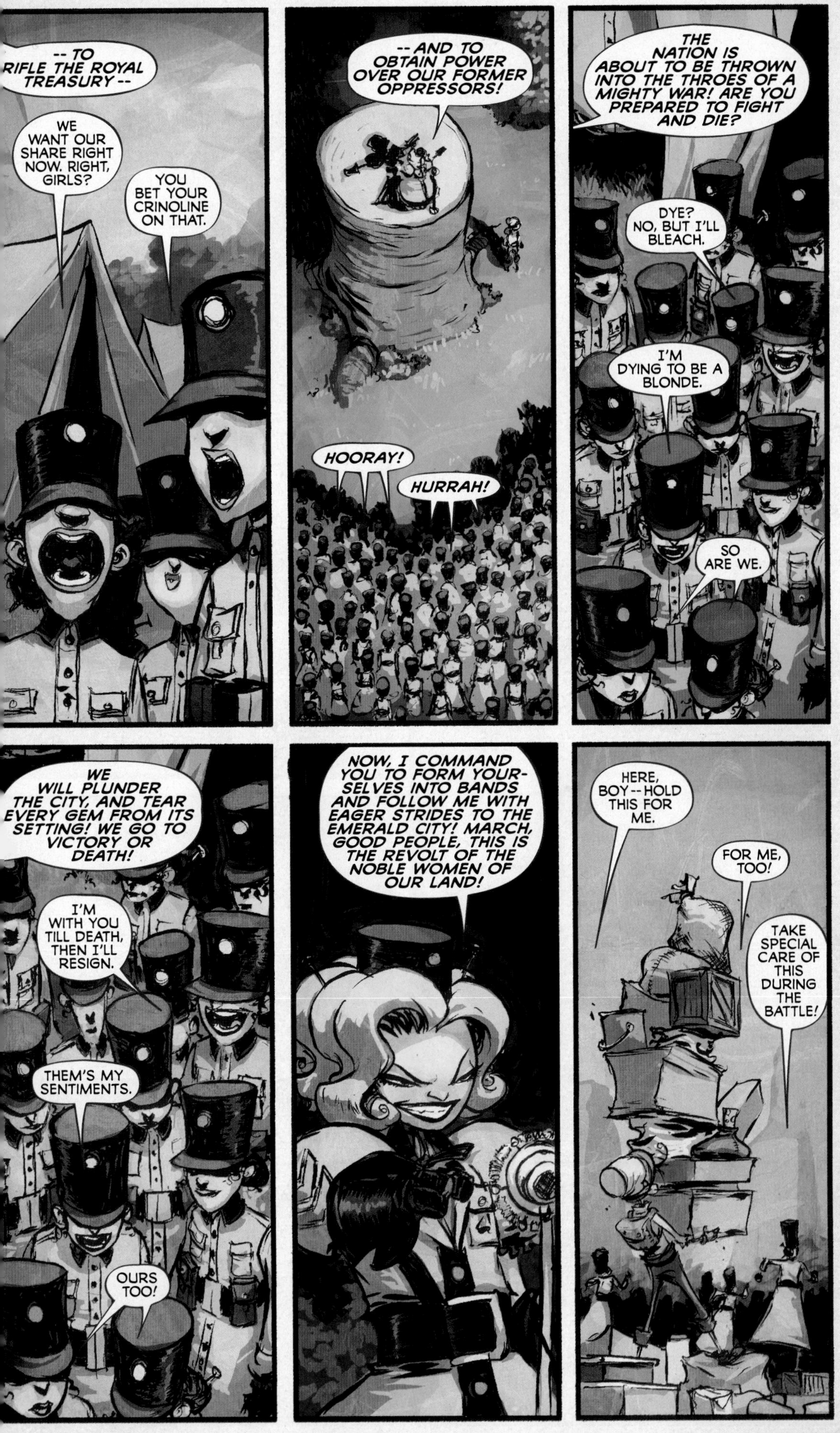
-- TO RIFLE THE ROYAL TREASURY --
WE WANT OUR SHARE RIGHT NOW. RIGHT, GIRLS?
YOU BET YOUR CRINOLINE ON THAT.
-- AND TO OBTAIN POWER OVER OUR FORMER OPPRESSORS!
HOORAY!
HURRAH!
THE NATION IS ABOUT TO BE THROWN INTO THE THROES OF A MIGHTY WAR! ARE YOU PREPARED TO FIGHT AND DIE?
DYE? NO, BUT I'LL BLEACH.
I'M DYING TO BE A BLONDE.
SO ARE WE.
WE WILL PLUNDER THE CITY, AND TEAR EVERY GEM FROM ITS SETTING! WE GO TO VICTORY OR DEATH!
I'M WITH YOU TILL DEATH, THEN I'LL RESIGN.
THEM'S MY SENTIMENTS.
OURS TOO!
NOW, I COMMAND YOU TO FORM YOURSELVES INTO BANDS AND FOLLOW ME WITH EAGER STRIDES TO THE EMERALD CITY! MARCH, GOOD PEOPLE, THIS IS THE REVOLT OF THE NOBLE WOMEN OF OUR LAND!
HERE, BOY--HOLD THIS FOR ME.
FOR ME, TOO!
TAKE SPECIAL CARE OF THIS DURING THE BATTLE!

HOW CURIOUS! HAS A CIRCUS COME TO TOWN?

GOOD MORNING, MY DEARS! WHAT CAN I DO FOR YOU?

SURRENDER INSTANTLY!

SURRENDER? WHY, IT'S SIMPLY IMPOSSIBLE -- AGAINST THE LAW! I NEVER HEARD OF SUCH A THING IN MY LIFE!

STILL, YOU MUST SURRENDER! WE ARE REVOLTING!

IT WAS NOT LONG BEFORE THEY CAME TO THE WALLS OF THE CITY.

YOU DON'T LOOK IT.

BUT WE ARE, AND WE MEAN TO CONQUER THE EMERALD CITY!

WHAT A NONSENSICAL IDEA! GO HOME TO YOUR MOTHERS AND YOUR WASH-TUBS, MY GOOD GIRLS, AND MILK THE COWS AND BAKE THE BREAD AND BE HAPPY.

ONCE MORE, DO YOU SURRENDER?

D-DON'T YOU KNOW IT'S A DANGEROUS THING TO CONQUER A CITY?

WE ARE NOT AFRAID!

THE DIE IS CAST! CHARGE, MY BRAVE GIRLS!

CREDIT TO WHOM CREDIT IS DUE!

AND, REMEMBER, NO QUARTER!

OOH! OW! MERCY!

OOWOO!

THE KEY, GIRLS!

CLICK

HALT!

WHY, WOULD YOU SHOOT A POOR, DEFENSELESS GIRL?

NO... MY GUN ISN'T LOADED.

NOT LOADED?

NO -- FOR FEAR OF ACCIDENTS. AND I'VE FORGOTTEN WHERE I HID THE POWDER AND SHOT. BUT IF YOU'LL WAIT, I'LL TRY TO HUNT THEM UP...

DON'T TROUBLE YOURSELF.

GIRLS, THE GUN ISN'T LOADED!

HOOORAAYYY

TIP FOLLOWED AFTER THE SOLDIER WITH THE GREEN WHISKERS...

...WHO REACHED THE PALACE BEFORE THE NEWS HAD SPREAD THAT THE CITY WAS CONQUERED.

TALLY ONE FOR ME!

OH, YOUR MAJESTY -- YOUR MAJESTY!

THE CITY IS *CONQUERED!* YOU ARE LOST -- *LOST* -- *LOST!*

THIS IS QUITE *SUDDEN!* WHO HAS CONQUERED ME?

A REGIMENT OF GIRLS, GATHERED FROM THE FOUR CORNERS OF THE LAND OF OZ.

BUT WHERE WAS MY STANDING ARMY AT THE TIME?

YOUR STANDING ARMY WAS RUNNING. NO MAN COULD FACE THE TERRIBLE WEAPONS OF THE INVADERS.

PLEASE GO AND BAR ALL THE DOORS AND WINDOWS OF THE PALACE, WHILE I SHOW THIS PUMPKIN-HEAD HOW TO THROW A QUOIT.

GOOD AFTERNOON, NOBLE PARENT! I'M GLAD TO SEE YOU'RE HERE. THAT TERRIBLE SAWHORSE RAN AWAY WITH ME.

DID YOU GET HURT? ARE YOU CRACKED AT ALL?

NO, I ARRIVED SAFELY. AND HIS MAJESTY HAS BEEN VERY KIND INDEED TO ME.

I DON'T MUCH MIND THE LOSS OF MY THRONE, FOR IT'S A TIRESOME JOB TO RULE OVER THE EMERALD CITY.

AND THIS CROWN IS SO HEAVY THAT IT MAKES MY HEAD ACHE.

BUT I HOPE THE CONQUERORS HAVE NO INTENTION OF INJURING ME, JUST BECAUSE I HAPPEN TO BE THE KING.

I HEARD THEM SAY THEY INTEND TO MAKE A RAG CARPET OF YOUR OUTSIDE AND STUFF THEIR SOFA-CUSHIONS WITH YOUR INSIDE.

THEN I'M REALLY IN DANGER. IT'LL BE WISE FOR ME TO CONSIDER A MEANS TO ESCAPE.

WHERE CAN YOU GO?

WHY, TO MY FRIEND THE TIN WOODMAN, WHO RULES OVER THE WINKIES, AND CALLS HIMSELF THEIR EMPEROR.

I'M SURE HE'LL PROTECT ME.

WILLY WILLY WALLY! WILLY WILLY WOE!

TIP! HE THOUGHT TO ESCAPE ME.

THOUGHT HE COULD RUN AWAY WITH MY PUMPKIN-HEAD AND MAGIC POWDER.

AH, NO, NO! HE COULDN'T CHEAT OLD MOMBI -- MOMBI THE *WITCH*, AH HA!

HEE HEE! I'LL GO TO THE EMERALD CITY AND PROMISE TO ASSIST THAT ARMY OF GIRLS BY MEANS OF MY WITCH-CRAFT...

...AND AFTERWARD THEY'LL TURN OVER TO ME TIP AND THE PUMPKIN-HEAD.

WILLY WILLY WOE!

IN THE EMERALD CITY --

THE PALACE IS SURROUNDED BY THE ENEMY. IT'S TOO LATE TO ESCAPE.

THEY'D SOON TEAR YOU TO PIECES.

IN AN EMERGENCY IT'S ALWAYS A GOOD THING TO PAUSE AND REFLECT. PLEASE EXCUSE ME WHILE I PAUSE AND REFLECT.

BUT WE'RE *ALL* IN DANGER! IF ANY OF THESE GIRLS UNDERSTAND COOKING, MY END ISN'T FAR OFF!

NONSENSE! THEY'RE TOO BUSY TO COOK EVEN IF THEY KNOW HOW.

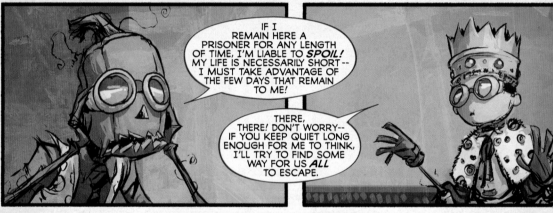

IF I REMAIN HERE A PRISONER FOR ANY LENGTH OF TIME, I'M LIABLE TO *SPOIL!* MY LIFE IS NECESSARILY SHORT-- I MUST TAKE ADVANTAGE OF THE FEW DAYS THAT REMAIN TO ME!

THERE, THERE! DON'T WORRY-- IF YOU KEEP QUIET LONG ENOUGH FOR ME TO THINK, I'LL TRY TO FIND SOME WAY FOR US *ALL* TO ESCAPE.

THE SCARE-CROW WALKED TO A CORNER AND STOOD FOR A GOOD FIVE MINUTES.

WHERE IS THE SAWHORSE YOU RODE HERE?

WHY, THE PUMPKINHEAD SAID HE WAS A JEWEL, SO I HAD HIM LOCKED UP IN THE ROYAL TREASURY. IT WAS THE ONLY PLACE I COULD THINK OF, YOUR MAJESTY.

EXCELLENT! BRING THE HORSE HERE AT ONCE.

PRESENTLY --

HE DOESN'T SEEM ESPECIALLY GRACEFUL... BUT I SUPPOSE HE CAN RUN?

HE CAN, INDEED!

THEN, BEARING US UPON HIS BACK, HE MUST DASH THROUGH THE RANKS OF THE REBELS AND CARRY US TO THE TIN WOOD-MAN.

HE CAN'T CARRY FOUR!

NO, BUT HE MAY BE INDUCED TO CARRY THREE. I SHALL THEREFORE LEAVE MY ROYAL ARMY BEHIND.

FOR, FROM THE EASE WITH WHICH HE WAS CONQUERED, I HAVE LITTLE CONFIDENCE IN HIS POWERS.

I EXPECTED THIS BLOW, BUT I CAN BEAR IT.

I SHALL DISGUISE MYSELF BY CUTTING OFF MY LOVELY GREEN WHISKERS.

FETCH A CLOTHESLINE AND TIE US ALL TOGETHER.

IF ONE FALLS OFF WE WILL ALL FALL OFF. IT'S WELL FOR ME TO BE CAREFUL, FOR MY VERY EXISTENCE IS IN DANGER.

I HAVE TO BE AS CAREFUL AS YOU DO.

NOT EXACTLY. IF ANYTHING HAPPENED TO ME, THAT WOULD BE THE END OF ME. BUT IF ANYTHING HAPPENED TO YOU, THEY COULD USE YOU FOR SEED.

NOW THROW OPEN THE GATES AND WE'LL MAKE A DASH TO LIBERTY OR TO DEATH.

SAWHORSE, YOU MUST SAVE US ALL. RUN AS FAST AS YOU CAN FOR THE GATE OF THE CITY, AND DON'T LET ANYTHING STOP YOU!

ALL RIGH

SL-SL-
SLOW H-HIM UP-
PUP-PUP-PUP! MY
STA-STRAW-WAW
IS ALL B-BEING
SH-SHAKE-
SHAKEN--

BUT THE SAW-HORSE'S
VIOLENT LEAPS SHOOK
THE BREATH OUT OF THE BOY
AND HE COULDN'T SPEAK.

SPA-LASH!

KEEP STILL, YOU FOOL SAWHORSE! *STOP STRUGGLING!*

WHAT DOES THAT WORD "FOOL" MEAN?

IT'S A TERM OF REPROACH. I ONLY USE IT WHEN I'M ANGRY.

THEN IT PLEASES ME TO CALL YOU A FOOL IN RETURN. I DIDN'T MAKE THE RIVER, NOR PUT IT IN OUR WAY. ONLY A TERM OF REPROACH IS FIT FOR ONE WHO BECOMES ANGRY WITH ME FOR FALLING IN.

I'LL ACKNOWLEDGE MYSELF IN THE WRONG. PADDLE WITH YOUR LEGS TOWARD THE SHORE.

THEY FINALLY REACHED THE OPPOSITE BANK.

ARE YOU ALL RIGHT, YOUR MAJESTY?

I'M ALL WRONG, SOME-HOW...

HOW VERY WET THIS WATER IS!

TIP MANAGED TO GET HIS KNIFE OUT.

PLOP

ARE YOU ALL RIGHT, JACK?

JACK! YOUR HEAD!

THERE IT IS!

THE PUMPKIN GENTLY BOBBED UP AND DOWN, BUT FLOATED NEARER AND STILL NEARER UNTIL --

DEAR ME! WHAT A DREADFUL EXPERIENCE!

I WONDER IF WATER IS LIABLE TO SPOIL PUMPKINS? IF IT IS, THEN MY DAYS ARE NUMBERED.

I'VE NEVER NOTICED THAT WATER SPOILS PUMPKINS... UNLESS THE WATER HAPPENS TO BE BOILING.

IF YOUR HEAD ISN'T CRACKED, YOU MUST BE IN FAIRLY GOOD CONDITION.

OH, MY HEAD ISN'T CRACKED IN THE LEAST.

THEN DON'T WORRY. CARE ONCE KILLED A CAT.

THEN I'M VERY GLAD INDEED THAT I'M NOT A CAT.

I WONDER IF HOT SUNSHINE IS LIABLE TO CRACK PUMPKINS.

NOT AT ALL! ALL YOU NEED FEAR, MY BOY, IS OLD AGE.

WHEN YOUR GOLDEN YOUTH IS DECAYED WE SHALL QUICKLY PART COMPANY -- BUT YOU NEEDN'T LOOK FORWARD TO IT. WE'LL DISCOVER THE FACT OURSELVES AND NOTIFY YOU.

THANK YOU VERY MUCH. THERE ARE DISTINCT ADVANTAGES IN BEING A SCARE-CROW.

IF ONE HAS FRIENDS NEAR AT HAND TO REPAIR DAMAGES, NOTHING VERY SERIOUS CAN HAPPEN TO YOU.

BUT COME! LET'S RESUME OUR JOURNEY. I'M ANXIOUS TO GREET MY FRIEND THE TIN WOODMAN.

I HOPE THAT HE RULES HIS PEOPLE MORE SUCCESSFULLY THAN I'VE RULED MINE.

GO SLOWLY, SAWHORSE. NOW THERE'S NO DANGER OF PURSUIT.

ALL RIGHT.

AREN'T YOU A LITTLE HOARSE?

SEE HERE, TIP-- CAN'T YOU PROTECT ME FROM INSULT?

I'M SURE JACK MEANT NO HARM.

I'LL HAVE NOTHING MORE TO DO WITH THAT PUMPKINHEAD -- HE LOSES HIS HEAD TOO EASILY.

*A*FTER A WHILE --

THIS REMINDS ME OF OLD TIMES. IT WAS UPON THIS KNOLL THAT NICK CHOPPER DESTROYED THE GRAY WOLVES OF THE WICKED WITCH OF THE WEST.

WHO WAS NICK CHOPPER?

THAT'S THE NAME OF THE TIN WOODMAN. NICK CHOPPER HAS THE BEST HEART IN ALL THE WORLD. I'M SURE HE'S PROVED AN EXCELLENT EMPEROR.

IS HE THE *EMPEROR* OF THE WINKIES?

YES, INDEED. THEY INVITED HIM TO RULE OVER THEM AFTER THE WICKED WITCH WAS DESTROYED.

I THOUGHT "EMPEROR" WAS THE TITLE OF A PERSON WHO RULES AN EMPIRE -- THE COUNTRY OF THE WINKIES IS ONLY A KINGDOM.

DON'T MENTION THAT TO THE TIN WOODMAN. YOU'D HURT HIS FEELINGS TERRIBLY. IT PLEASES HIM TO BE TERMED EMPEROR RATHER THAN KING.

IT MAKES NO DIFFERENCE TO ME.

AND HERE IS WHERE I ONCE SAVED DOROTHY FROM THE WITCH'S CROWS.

DO CROWS INJURE PUMPKINS?

THEY ARE ALL DEAD, SO IT DOESN'T MATTER.

HERE IS WHERE THE WINGED MONKEYS ATTACKED US, AND FLEW AWAY WITH LITTLE DOROTHY.

DO WINGED MONKEYS EVER EAT PUMPKINS?

YOU HAVE LITTLE CAUSE TO WORRY. THE WINGED MONKEYS ARE SLAVES OF THE GOLDEN CAP, AND ONLY ATTACKED US BECAUSE THE WICKED WITCH COMMANDED THEM.

I'M DREADFULLY HUNGRY!

I HOPE YOU'RE NOT FOND OF EATING PUMPKINS.

NOT UNLESS THEY'RE STEWED AND MADE INTO PIES.

WHAT A *COWARD* THAT PUMPKIN-HEAD IS!

YOU MIGHT BE A COWARD YOURSELF, IF YOU KNEW YOU WERE LIABLE TO SPOIL!

THERE, THERE! WE ALL HAVE OUR WEAKNESSES, FRIENDS.

I'M TIRED OUT, TOO! YAWW-AWW!

IT WAS THE SAME WAY WITH LITTLE DOROTHY. WE ALWAYS HAD TO SIT THROUGH THE NIGHT WHILE SHE SLEPT.

I NEVER SLEEP.

I DON'T EVEN KNOW WHAT SLEEP IS.

SINCE THIS BOY IS HUNGRY AND HAS NOTHING TO EAT, LET'S ALLOW HIM TO SLEEP. IT'S SAID THAT IN SLEEP A MORTAL MAY FORGET EVEN HUNGER.

YOUR MAJESTY IS AS GOOD AS YOU ARE WISE -- AND THAT'S SAYING A GOOD DEAL!

TIP AWOKE SOON AFTER DAWN.

I PLUCKED THESE RIPE BERRIES FROM SOME BUSHES NEAR BY.

THANK YOU.

THE SAW-HORSE ROCKED AND ROLLED OVER THE FLOWER-STREWN FIELDS AND CARRIED ITS RIDERS SWIFTLY UPON THEIR WAY.

AFTER AN HOUR'S RIDE--

LOOK -- THE EMPEROR'S PALACE! HOW DELIGHTED I'LL BE TO SEE MY OLD FRIEND THE TIN WOOD-MAN AGAIN.

SHOW US AT ONCE TO YOUR MASTER, THE EMPEROR.

I MUST ASK YOU TO WAIT. THIS IS HIS MAJESTY'S DAY FOR BEING POLISHED. JUST NOW HIS AUGUST PRESENCE IS THICKLY SMEARED WITH PUTZ-POMADE.

OH, I SEE! BUT SHOW US IN -- I'M SURE THE EMPEROR WILL RECEIVE US, EVEN IN HIS PRESENT STATE.

MY FRIEND WAS EVER INCLINED TO BE A DANDY. I SUPPOSE HE'S MORE PROUD THAN EVER OF HIS PERSONAL APPEARANCE.

HE IS, INDEED.

OUR MIGHTY EMPEROR HAS LATELY CAUSED HIMSELF TO BE NICKEL-PLATED.

GOOD GRACIOUS! IF HIS WIT BEARS THE SAME POLISH, HOW SPARKLING IT MUST BE!

THE EMPEROR'S STATE IS ALWAYS MAGNIFICENT. I'LL TELL HIM OF YOUR ARRIVAL.

WELL! WELL! WELL!

WHAT A GREAT SURPRISE!

MY DEAR OLD FRIEND! MY NOBLE COMRADE! HOW DELIGHTED I AM TO MEET YOU ONCE AGAIN!

DEAR ME! WHAT A MESS I'M IN.

NEVER MIND, MY FRIEND. I'LL SEND YOU TO MY IMPERIAL LAUNDRY, AND YOU'LL COME OUT GOOD AS NEW.

WON'T I BE MANGLED?

NO, INDEED! BUT TELL ME, HOW DID YOUR MAJESTY COME HERE, AND WHO ARE YOUR COMPANIONS?

*T*HE SCARECROW INTRODUCED TIP AND JACK PUMPKINHEAD.

I HOPE YOU'RE ENJOYING GOOD HEALTH?

I THANK YOUR MAJESTY, BUT I AM IN CONSTANT TERROR OF THE DAY WHEN I SHALL SPOIL.

NONSENSE!

BEFORE YOUR HEAD HAS TIME TO SPOIL YOU CAN HAVE IT CANNED -- THAT WAY IT MAY BE PRESERVED INDEFINITELY.

THE TIN WOODMAN BEGGED HIS FRIENDS TO EXCUSE HIM WHILE HE ALLOWED HIS SERVANTS TO FINISH POLISHING HIM.

MAGNIFICENT! I CONGRATULATE YOU ON YOUR IMPROVED APPEARANCE.

THE NICKELPLATE WAS A HAPPY THOUGHT. I'D BECOME SOMEWHAT SCRATCHED DURING MY ADVENTUROUS EXPERIENCES.

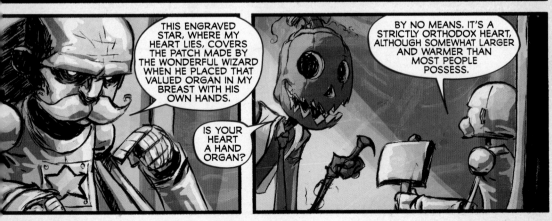

THIS ENGRAVED STAR, WHERE MY HEART LIES, COVERS THE PATCH MADE BY THE WONDERFUL WIZARD WHEN HE PLACED THAT VALUED ORGAN IN MY BREAST WITH HIS OWN HANDS.

IS YOUR HEART A HAND ORGAN?

BY NO MEANS. IT'S A STRICTLY ORTHODOX HEART, ALTHOUGH SOMEWHAT LARGER AND WARMER THAN MOST PEOPLE POSSESS.

NICK, MY FRIEND -- THE GIRLS OF OZ HAVE RISEN IN REVOLT AND DRIVEN ME OUT OF THE EMERALD CITY.

GREAT GOODNESS! THEY SURELY DON'T COMPLAIN OF YOUR WISE AND GRACIOUS RULE?

THEY SAY IT'S A POOR RULE THAT DOESN'T WORK BOTH WAYS. THESE FEMALES ARE OF THE OPINION THAT MEN HAVE RULED LONG ENOUGH.

SO THEY'VE CAPTURED MY CITY, ROBBED IT OF ALL ITS JEWELS, AND ARE RUNNING THINGS TO SUIT THEMSELVES.

I HEARD THEM SAY THAT THEY INTEND TO MARCH HERE AND CAPTURE THE CASTLE AND CITY OF THE TIN WOODMAN.

DEAR ME! WE MUSTN'T GIVE THEM TIME TO DO THAT. WE'LL GO AT ONCE AND RECAPTURE THE EMERALD CITY AND PLACE THE SCARE-CROW AGAIN UPON HIS THRONE.

I WAS SURE YOU'D HELP ME. HOW LARGE AN ARMY CAN YOU ASSEMBLE?

WE DON'T NEED AN ARMY! WE FOUR, WITH THE AID OF MY GLEAMING AXE, ARE ENOUGH TO STRIKE TERROR INTO THE HEARTS OF THE REBELS.

WE FIVE.

FIVE?

YES, THE SAW-HORSE IS BRAVE AND FEARLESS.

I BEGIN TO THINK THAT WONDERS WILL NEVER CEASE!

HOW DID THIS CREATURE COME TO BE ALIVE?

I DID IT WITH A MAGIC POWDER. THE SAW-HORSE HAS BEEN VERY USEFUL.

HE ENABLED US TO ESCAPE THE REBELS.

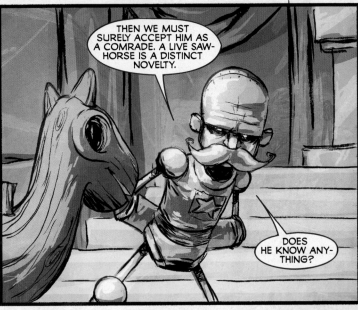

THEN WE MUST SURELY ACCEPT HIM AS A COMRADE. A LIVE SAW-HORSE IS A DISTINCT NOVELTY.

DOES HE KNOW ANY-THING?

I CAN'T CLAIM GREAT EXPERIENCE, BUT OFTEN IT OCCURS TO ME THAT I KNOW MORE THAN THOSE AROUND ME.

PERHAPS YOU DO, FOR EXPERIENCE DOESN'T ALWAYS MEAN WISDOM.

*T*HEY QUICKLY MADE PREPARATIONS TO START UPON THEIR JOURNEY.

THE SCARECROW WAS TAKEN APART AND CLEANED.

THE PAINTED SACK THAT SERVED HIM FOR A HEAD WAS LAUNDERED...

...AND RESTUFFED WITH THE BRAINS ORIGINALLY GIVEN HIM BY THE GREAT WIZARD.

HIS CROWN WAS AGAIN SEWED ON.

ALTHOUGH I'M IN NO WAY ADDICTED TO VANITY, I'M QUITE PLEASED WITH MYSELF.

MEANWHILE, TIP MENDED JACK'S WOODEN LIMBS.

NEXT MORNING THEY SET OUT UPON THE RETURN JOURNEY TO THE EMERALD CITY.

*G*ENERAL JINJUR WAS VERY UNEASY ABOUT THE ESCAPE OF THE SCARECROW FROM THE EMERALD CITY.

JINJUR, MY BOY TIP HAS RUN AWAY WITH THE PUMPKINHEAD AND I'VE GOT TO --

HOW DARE YOU CUT IN WITH YOUR PRIVATE GRIEFS WHILE THE NATION IS IN THE THROES OF A MIGHTY WAR?

LOOK HERE, I'VE DISCOVERED THAT THE SCARECROW AND THE TIN WOODMAN HAVE JOINED FORCES. THAT MEANS DANGER TO YOU AND YOUR ENTIRE ARMY.

IF YOU'LL TURN TIP OVER TO ME, I'LL INVOKE MY POWERS OF MAGIC TO ASSIST YOU, GIRL.

GIRL! I AM THE *QUEEN*, UNDERSTAND? *QUEEN OF THE EMERALD CITY*, YOU UGLY OLD WITCH!

WHAT! BY THE POWER OF MY MYSTIC ART I'LL DRAG YOU DOWN, DOWN, *DOWN* FROM YOUR THRONE. I'LL TURN YOU INTO A WRITHING CATERPILLAR!

FIZZLE-FOOZLE-FI--

OH, SPARE ME! SPARE ME! I'LL PROMISE YOU LARGE REWARDS!

THAT'S BETTER. AND I'M *NOT* AN UGLY OLD WITCH, AM I? I'M A VERY *BEAUTIFUL* WITCH, AM I NOT?

SAY IT!

N-N-NO-O-O, YOU'RE NOT OLD. I THINK YOU'RE VERY BEAUTIFUL.

HEE HEE! THAT'S A DEARIE.

NOW, I'LL USE MY POWERS TO PREVENT THE RETURN OF THE SCARECROW AND HIS COMPANIONS--

I WANT YOU TO *DESTROY* THEM ALL.

NO, NO. NOT TIP. NOT TIP. I'LL DO AN INCANTATION THAT WILL DEFEAT THE SCARE-CROW AND TIN WOOD-MAN, BUT AFTER-WARD --

YES, YES. AFTERWARD YOU'LL GET YOUR TIP.

*M*OMBI RETIRED TO A SMALL ROOM HIGH UP IN A TOWER AND LOCKED HERSELF IN.

HATEFUL THING!

VERY CURIOUS. I OUGHT TO KNOW BY HEART EVERY STEP OF THIS JOURNEY, YET I FEAR WE'VE LOST OUR WAY.

THAT'S QUITE IMPOSSIBLE. WHY DO YOU THINK THAT WE'VE LOST OUR WAY?

HERE'S A GREAT FIELD OF SUNFLOWERS -- AND I NEVER SAW THIS FIELD BEFORE IN ALL MY LIFE.

BUT WHERE DID THESE FLOWERS COME FROM? AND...

...AND WHAT ARE THEY DOING?

IT'S WITCH-CRAFT!

HAH!

HAHAHAHAHAHAHAHAHAHA

STOP! THEY'RE ALIVE! THEY'RE GIRLS!

IT WOULD BE HEARTLESS TO CHOP DOWN THESE PRETTY CREATURES. YET I DON'T KNOW HOW ELSE WE CAN PROCEED UPON OUR WAY.

THEY LOOKED STRANGELY LIKE THE FACES OF THE ARMY OF REVOLT.

I SUSPECT THIS IS A TRICK OF OLD MOMBI'S TO TRY TO STOP US. PROBABLY IT'S NOTHING MORE THAN AN ILLUSION, AND THERE ARE NO SUNFLOWERS AT ALL.

THEN LET'S SHUT OUR EYES AND WALK FORWARD.

CAN'T I PICK A BOUQUET?

MY EYES AREN'T PAINTED TO SHUT. BECAUSE YOU HAPPEN TO HAVE TIN EYELIDS, YOU MUSTN'T IMAGINE WE'RE ALL BUILT IN THE SAME WAY.

THE EYES OF THE SAW-HORSE ARE KNOT EYES.

NEVERTHELESS, YOU MUST RIDE QUICKLY FORWARD. WE'LL FOLLOW AND TRY TO ESCAPE. MY EYES ARE SO DAZZLED THAT I CAN SCARCELY SEE.

*T*IP GRABBED THE STUB TAIL OF THE SAW-HORSE AND THE PUMPKINHEAD RODE BOLDLY FORWARD.

FATHER! THE WAY'S CLEAR!

NOT A TRACE.

THEY PROCEEDED UPON THEIR JOURNEY, BUT OLD MOMBI HAD SO CHANGED THE APPEARANCE OF THE LANDSCAPE THAT THEY WOULD HAVE BEEN LOST IF NOT FOR THE SCARECROW.

SOMEONE'S PLAYED A TRICK UPON US.

I'VE KNOWN OLD MOMBI TO DO THINGS LIKE THAT BEFORE.

LET'S TAKE OUR DIRECTION FROM THE SUN. NO WITCHCRAFT CAN CHANGE THE COURSE OF THE SUN, SO THEREFORE IT'S A SAFE GUIDE.

SNAP!

OH!

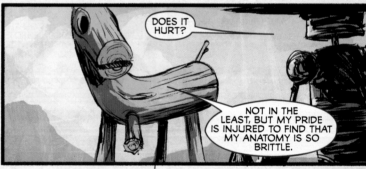

DOES IT HURT?

NOT IN THE LEAST, BUT MY PRIDE IS INJURED TO FIND THAT MY ANATOMY IS SO BRITTLE.

IF THERE WERE TREES NEARBY I MIGHT SOON MANUFACTURE ANOTHER LEG FOR THIS ANIMAL, BUT I CAN'T SEE EVEN A SHRUB FOR MILES.

LET'S ALL THINK, AND PERHAPS WE'LL FIND A WAY TO REPAIR THE SAW-HORSE.

I MUST START MY BRAINS WORKING -- EXPERIENCE HAS TAUGHT ME THAT I CAN DO ANYTHING IF I TAKE TIME TO THINK IT OUT.

WHAT SORT OF CREATURE IS THAT APPROACHING US?

GOOD MORNING.

GOOD MORNING, ONE AND ALL. I HOPE YOU ARE, AS AN AGGREGATION, ENJOYING EXCELLENT HEALTH.

PERMIT ME TO PRESENT MY CARD.

"MR. H. M. WOGGLE-BUG, T. E."

Mr.
H. M. Woggle-Bug,
T. E.

DEAR ME!

HOW VERY PECULIAR!

ARE YOU REALLY A WOGGLE-BUG?

MOST CERTAINLY, MY DEAR SIR. IS NOT MY NAME UPON THE CARD?

IT IS -- BUT MAY I ASK WHAT "H. M." STANDS FOR?

"H. M." MEANS HIGHLY MAGNIFIED.

I SEE. AND ARE YOU, IN TRUTH, HIGHLY MAGNIFIED?

SIR, I TAKE YOU FOR A GENTLEMAN OF JUDGMENT AND DISCERNMENT.

DOES IT NOT OCCUR TO YOU THAT I AM SEVERAL THOUSAND TIMES *GREATER* THAN ANY WOGGLE-BUG YOU EVER SAW BEFORE?

THEREFORE IT IS PLAINLY EVIDENT THAT I AM HIGHLY MAGNIFIED, AND THERE IS NO GOOD REASON WHY YOU SHOULD DOUBT THE FACT.

PARDON ME, WOULD IT BE IMPROPER TO ASK WHAT THE "T. E." STANDS FOR?

THOSE LETTERS EXPRESS MY DEGREE. TO BE MORE EXPLICIT, THE INITIALS MEAN THAT I AM THOROUGHLY EDUCATED.

I CONFESS THAT YOUR ABRUPT APPEARANCE HAS SURPRISED ME. I HOPE THAT THIS DOESN'T DISTRESS YOU --

DO NOT APOLOGIZE, I BEG OF YOU!

IT AFFORDS ME GREAT PLEASURE TO SURPRISE PEOPLE, FOR SURELY I CANNOT BE CLASSED WITH ORDINARY INSECTS.

IT IS BUT HONEST THAT I SHOULD ACKNOWLEDGE THAT I WAS BORN AN ORDINARY WOGGLE-BUG.

IF YOU WILL PERMIT ME TO SEAT MYSELF IN YOUR AUGUST COMPANY, I WILL GLADLY RELATE MY HISTORY, SO THAT YOU WILL BETTER COMPREHEND MY UNUSUAL -- MAY I SAY REMARKABLE? -- APPEARANCE.

"KNOWING NO BETTER, I USED MY ARMS AS WELL AS MY LEGS FOR WALKING, AND CRAWLED UNDER STONES OR HID AMONG GRASSES...

"...WITH NO THOUGHT BEYOND FINDING A FEW INSECTS SMALLER THAN MYSELF TO FEED UPON.

"THE CHILL NIGHTS RENDERED ME STIFF AND MOTIONLESS -- BUT EACH MORNING THE WARM RAYS OF THE SUN RESTORED ME TO ACTIVITY."

"BUT DESTINY HAD SINGLED ME OUT, HUMBLE THOUGH I WAS, FOR A GRANDER FATE! ONE DAY I CRAWLED NEAR TO A COUNTRY SCHOOL-HOUSE. MY CURIOSITY BEING EXCITED, I MADE BOLD TO ENTER.

"IN FRONT OF A HEARTH OF GLOWING EMBERS, SAT THE MASTER AT HIS DESK.

"WHEN I FOUND THAT THE HEARTH WAS WARMER THAN THE SUNSHINE, I RESOLVED TO ESTABLISH MY HOME BESIDE IT.

"I FOUND A CHARMING NEST BETWEEN TWO BRICKS AND HID MYSELF THEREIN FOR MANY MONTHS.

"PROFESSOR NOWITALL IS, DOUBTLESS, THE MOST FAMOUS SCHOLAR IN THE LAND OF OZ.

"NOT ONE PUPIL WAS MORE ATTENTIVE TO HIS LECTURES THAN THE HUMBLE WOGGLE-BUG. I ACQUIRED A MARVELOUS FUND OF KNOWLEDGE."

THAT IS WHY I PLACE "T. E." -- THOROUGHLY EDUCATED -- UPON MY CARDS.

EDUCATION IS A THING TO BE PROUD OF. THE BRAINS GIVEN ME BY THE GREAT WIZARD ARE CONSIDERED BY MY FRIENDS TO BE UNEXCELLED.

A GOOD HEART IS, I BELIEVE, MUCH MORE DESIRABLE THAN EDUCATION OR BRAINS.

TO ME, A GOOD LEG IS MORE DESIRABLE THAN EITHER.

COULD SEEDS BE CONSIDERED IN THE LIGHT OF BRAINS?

KEEP QUIET!

I MUST HAVE LIVED FULLY THREE YEARS IN THAT SECLUDED SCHOOL-HOUSE HEARTH, DRINKING THIRSTILY OF THE EVER-FLOWING FONT OF LIMPID KNOWLEDGE.

QUITE POETICAL.

"BUT ONE DAY A MARVELOUS CIRCUMSTANCE ALTERED MY VERY EXISTENCE AND BROUGHT ME TO MY PRESENT PINNACLE OF GREATNESS."

MY DEAR CHILDREN, I'VE CAPTURED A VERY RARE AND INTERESTING SPECIMEN. DO ANY OF YOU KNOW WHAT A WOGGLE-BUG IS?

NO!

I'LL GET OUT MY FAMOUS MAGNIFYING GLASS AND THROW THE INSECT UPON A SCREEN IN A HIGHLY-MAGNIFIED CONDITION, THAT YOU MAY STUDY HIS PECULIARITIES.

"HE BROUGHT FROM A CUPBOARD A MOST CURIOUS INSTRUMENT..."

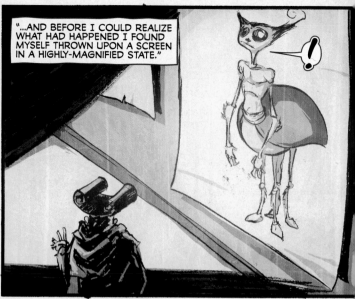

"...AND BEFORE I COULD REALIZE WHAT HAD HAPPENED I FOUND MYSELF THROWN UPON A SCREEN IN A HIGHLY-MAGNIFIED STATE."

BEHOLD -- THIS HIGHLY-MAGNIFIED WOGGLE-BUG -- ONE OF THE MOST CURIOUS INSECTS IN EXISTENCE!

"BEING THOROUGHLY EDUCATED, AND KNOWING WHAT IS REQUIRED OF A CULTURED GENTLEMAN, I MADE A POLITE BOW."

"MY ACTION MUST HAVE STARTLED THEM..."

EEEEE!

"...FOR TWO LITTLE GIRLS PERCHED UPON THE WINDOW-SILL FELL BACKWARD OUT OF THE WINDOW. THE PROFESSOR RUSHED AWAY TO SEE IF THE POOR CHILDREN WERE INJURED."

AAA!

I WAS LEFT ALONE, STILL IN A HIGHLY MAGNIFIED STATE. IT IMMEDIATELY OCCURRED TO ME THAT THIS WAS A GOOD OPPORTUNITY TO ESCAPE.

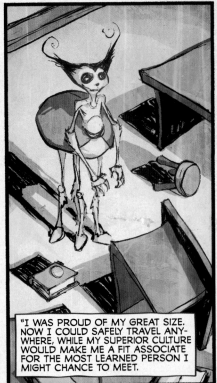

"I WAS PROUD OF MY GREAT SIZE. NOW I COULD SAFELY TRAVEL ANYWHERE, WHILE MY SUPERIOR CULTURE WOULD MAKE ME A FIT ASSOCIATE FOR THE MOST LEARNED PERSON I MIGHT CHANCE TO MEET."

"SO I CALMLY WALKED OUT OF THE SCHOOL-HOUSE AND ESCAPED UNNOTICED."

I NEVER CEASE TO CONGRATULATE MYSELF FOR ESCAPING WHILE HIGHLY MAGNIFIED, FOR MY EXCESSIVE KNOWLEDGE WOULD HAVE PROVED OF LITTLE USE HAD I REMAINED AN INSIGNIFICANT BUG.

I DIDN'T KNOW BEFORE THAT INSECTS WORE CLOTHES.

NOR DO THEY, IN THEIR NATURAL STATE. BUT I HAD THE GOOD FORTUNE TO SAVE THE NINTH LIFE OF A TAILOR -- TAILORS HAVING, LIKE CATS, NINE LIVES.

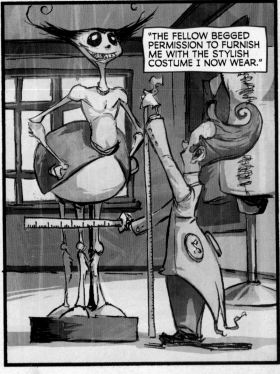

"THE FELLOW BEGGED PERMISSION TO FURNISH ME WITH THE STYLISH COSTUME I NOW WEAR."

IT FITS VERY NICELY, DOES IT NOT?

HE MUST HAVE BEEN A GOOD TAILOR.

HE WAS A GOOD-*HEARTED* TAILOR, AT ANY RATE.

BUT WHERE WERE YOU GOING WHEN YOU MET US?

I INTENDED TO VISIT THE EMERALD CITY TO GIVE A COURSE OF LECTURES ON THE "ADVANTAGES OF MAGNIFICATION."

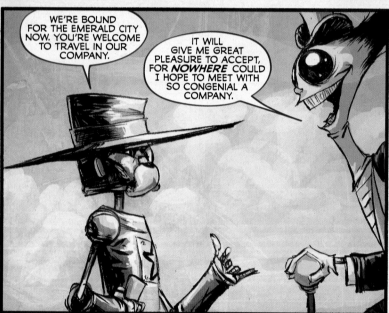

WE'RE BOUND FOR THE EMERALD CITY NOW. YOU'RE WELCOME TO TRAVEL IN OUR COMPANY.

IT WILL GIVE ME GREAT PLEASURE TO ACCEPT, FOR *NOWHERE* COULD I HOPE TO MEET WITH SO CONGENIAL A COMPANY.

WE ARE QUITE AS CONGENIAL AS FLIES AND HONEY.

BUT -- PARDON ME -- ARE YOU NOT ALL RATHER -- AHEM! -- RATHER *UNUSUAL*?

EVERYTHING IN LIFE IS UNUSUAL UNTIL YOU GET ACCUSTOMED TO IT.

WHAT RARE PHILOSOPHY!

YES, MY BRAINS ARE WORKING WELL TODAY.

THEN LET US BEND OUR STEPS TOWARD THE EMERALD CITY.

THE SAW-HORSE HAS BROKEN A LEG, SO HE *CAN'T* BEND HIS STEPS. THERE'S NO WOOD AROUND -- AND WE CAN'T LEAVE THE HORSE BEHIND BECAUSE THE PUMPKINHEAD HAS TO RIDE.

IF THE PUMPKINHEAD IS TO RIDE, WHY NOT USE ONE OF *HIS* LEGS TO MAKE A LEG FOR THE HORSE? I JUDGE THAT BOTH ARE MADE OF WOOD.

I WONDER WHY MY BRAINS DID NOT THINK OF THAT! GET TO WORK, MY DEAR NICK.

JACK SUBMITTED TO HAVING HIS LEFT LEG AMPUTATED.

IT'S A DISGRACE TO A RESPECTABLE SAW-HORSE.

I BEG YOU TO BE MORE CAREFUL IN YOUR SPEECH. REMEMBER THAT IT'S MY LEG YOU'RE ABUSING.

I CANNOT FORGET IT, FOR IT'S QUITE AS FLIMSY AS THE REST OF YOUR PERSON.

FLIMSY! ME FLIMSY! HOW DARE YOU CALL ME FLIMSY?

YOU'RE BUILT AS ABSURDLY AS A JUMPING-JACK. EVEN YOUR HEAD WON'T STAY STRAIGHT!

FRIENDS, I ENTREAT YOU NOT TO QUARREL! WE'RE NONE OF US ABOVE CRITICISM, SO LET'S BEAR WITH EACH OTHER'S FAULTS.

AN EXCELLENT SUGGESTION. YOU MUST HAVE AN EXCELLENT HEART, MY METALLIC FRIEND.

I HAVE. MY HEART IS QUITE THE BEST PART OF ME.

*T*HEN THEY STARTED AGAIN IN THE DIRECTION OF THE EMERALD CITY.

THEY SOON DISCOVERED THAT THE SAW-HORSE LIMPED.

HIS NEW LEG'S A TRIFLE TOO LONG.

I'LL CHOP IT DOWN WITH MY AXE.

IT'S A SHAME I BROKE MY OTHER LEG.

ON THE CONTRARY, YOU SHOULD CONSIDER THE ACCIDENT MOST FORTUNATE. FOR A HORSE IS NEVER OF MUCH USE UNTIL HE HAS BEEN BROKEN.

I BEG YOUR PARDON -- YOUR JOKE IS A POOR ONE, AND AS OLD AS IT IS POOR.

A JOKE DERIVED FROM A PLAY UPON WORDS IS CONSIDERED AMONG EDUCATED PEOPLE TO BE EMINENTLY PROPER.

WHAT DOES THAT MEAN?

IT MEANS THAT OUR LANGUAGE CONTAINS MANY WORDS HAVING A DOUBLE MEANING.

TO PRONOUNCE A JOKE THAT ALLOWS BOTH MEANINGS OF A WORD PROVES THE JOKER A PERSON OF CULTURE, WHO HAS A THOROUGH COMMAND OF THE LANGUAGE.

I DON'T BELIEVE THAT. *ANYBODY* CAN MAKE A PUN.

NOT SO. IT REQUIRES EDUCATION OF A HIGH ORDER. ARE YOU EDUCATED, YOUNG SIR?

NOT ESPECIALLY.

THEN YOU CANNOT JUDGE. I MYSELF AM THOROUGHLY EDUCATED, AND I SAY THAT PUNS DISPLAY GENIUS.

FOR INSTANCE, WERE I TO RIDE UPON THIS SAW-HORSE, H WOULD NOT ONLY BE AN ANIMAL HE WOULD BECOME AN EQUIPAG FOR HE WOULD THEN BE A HORSE-AND-BUGGY.

UGH!

HMPH!

WHAT DID THE WOGGLE-BUG SAY?

ALTHOUGH I HAVE A HIGH RESPECT FOR BRAINS, I BEGIN SUSPECT THAT YOURS ARE TIGHTLY TANGLED. I MUST BEG YOU TO RESTRAIN YOUR SUPERIOR EDUCATION WHILE IN OUR SOCIETY.

WE'RE NOT VERY PARTICULAR, AND WE'RE *EXCEEDINGLY* KIND-HEARTED. BUT IF YOUR SUPERIOR CULTURE GETS LEAKY AGAIN...

I WILL ENDEAVOR TO RESTRAIN MYSELF.

THAT'S ALL WE CAN EXPECT.

WHEN THEY STOPPED TO ALLOW TIP TO REST...

THIS MUST BE VILLAGE OF THE FIELD MICE.

I WONDER IF MY OLD FRIEND, THE QUEEN OF THE FIELD MICE, IS IN THIS NEIGHBORHOOD.

WHEEET

GOOD DAY, YOUR MAJESTY. I TRUST YOU'RE ENJOYING GOOD HEALTH?

THANK YOU, I'M QUIT[E] WELL. CAN I D[O] ANYTHING TO ASSIST MY OL[D] FRIENDS?

YOU CAN, INDEED. LET ME TAKE A DOZEN OF YOUR SUBJECTS WITH ME TO THE EMERALD CITY.

WILL THEY BE INJURED IN ANY WAY?

I THINK NOT. I'LL CARRY THEM HIDDEN IN THE STRAW WHICH STUFFS MY BODY.

WHEN I UNBUTTON MY JACKET, THEY HA[VE] ONLY TO RUSH OUT AND SCAMPER HOME.

BY DOING THIS THEY'LL ASSIST ME TO REGAIN MY THRONE, WHICH THE ARMY OF REVOLT HAS TAKEN FROM ME.

IN THAT CASE, WHENEVER YOU'RE READY, I'LL CALL TWELVE OF MY MOST INTELLIGENT SUBJECTS.

I'M READY NOW.

SQUEEE!

W HAT THE QUEEN SAID TO THE DOZEN FIELD MICE WAS IN THE MOUSE LANGUAGE.

HEY OBEYED WITHOUT HESITATION.

HANK YOU.

ONE MORE THING YOU MIGHT DO TO SERVE US -- RUN AHEAD AND SHOW US THE WAY TO THE EMERALD CITY.

SOME ENEMY IS EVIDENTLY TRYING TO PREVENT US FROM REACHING IT.

I'LL DO THAT GLADLY. ARE YOU READY?

I'M RESTED. LET'S START.

THEY RESUMED THEIR JOURNEY.

THAT RIVER THREATENS TO BAR OUR WAY.

LOOK -- THE QUEEN'S GOING STEADILY ON. FOLLOW HER!

MANY WERE THE OBSTACLES THROWN IN THEIR WAY BY THE ARTS OF OLD MOMBI. YET NOT ONE OF THE OBSTACLES REALLY EXISTED -- ALL WERE CLEVERLY CONTRIVED DECEPTIONS.

WE'LL PASS THROUGH IN SAFETY!

AND WITHOUT ENCOUNTERING A SINGLE DROP OF WATER!

THEN A WALL OF GRANITE OPPOSED THEIR ADVANCE.

THE FIELD MOUSE IS WALKING STRAIGHT THROUGH IT.

THE WALL IS MELTING INTO MIST!

AFTERWARD, THEY SAW ROADS BRANCHING OFF IN DIFFERENT DIRECTIONS.

THESE ROADS ARE ALL STRANGE.

WHAT A LOT OF THEM THERE ARE!

THE ROADS BEGAN WHIRLING AROUND LIKE A MIGHTY WHEEL, FIRST IN ONE DIRECTION AND THEN IN THE OTHER.

B-BE-WILDERING...

FOLLOW ME!

WHEN THEY'D GONE A FEW PACES...

THE WHIRLING PATHWAYS VANISHED!

ZOMBI'S LAST TRICK WAS THE MOST FEARFUL OF ALL.

IF THAT FIRE REACHES ME I'LL BE GONE IN NO TIME!

I'M OFF, TOO!

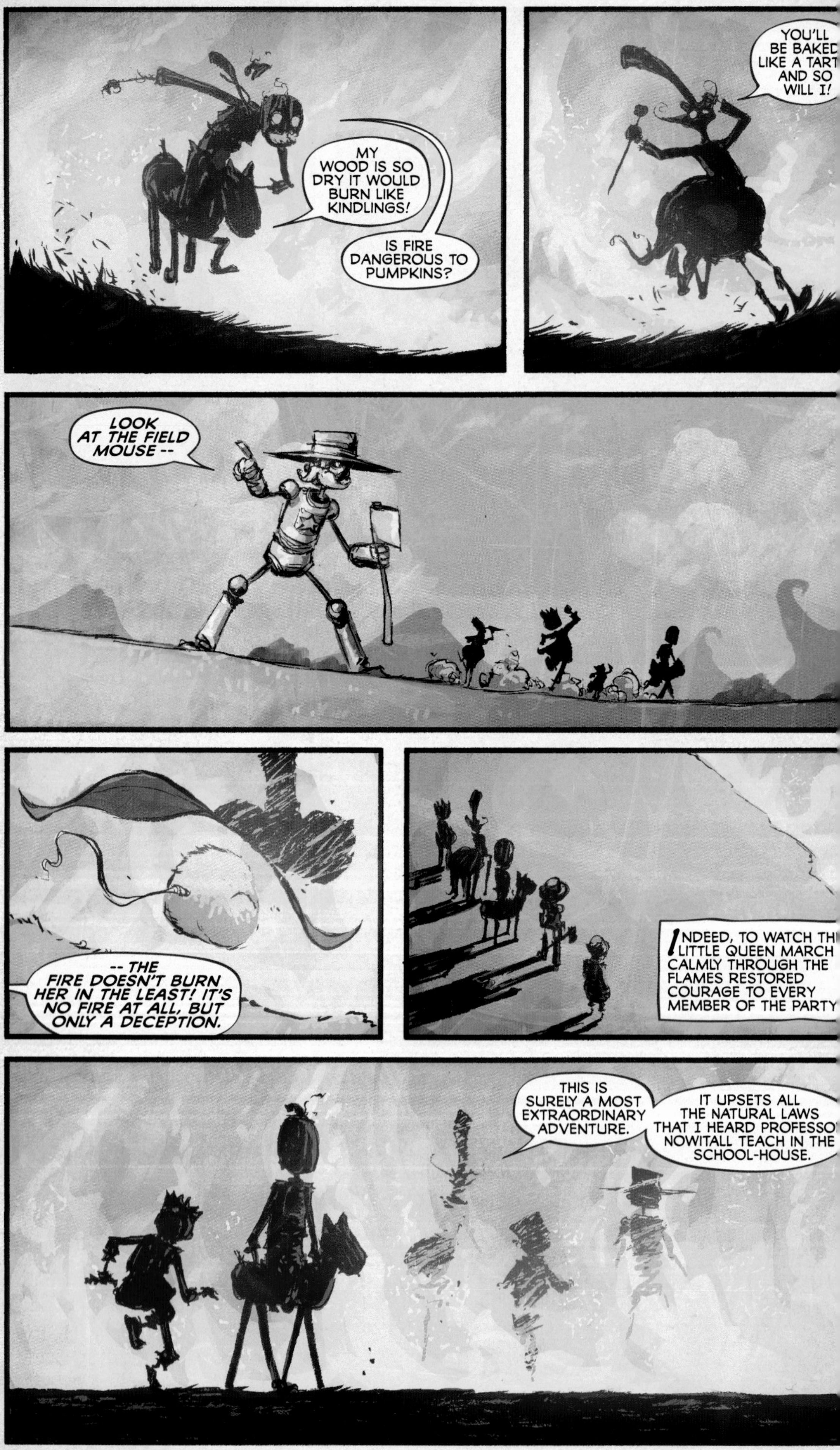
MY WOOD IS SO DRY IT WOULD BURN LIKE KINDLINGS!
IS FIRE DANGEROUS TO PUMPKINS?
YOU'LL BE BAKED LIKE A TART AND SO WILL I!
LOOK AT THE FIELD MOUSE --
-- THE FIRE DOESN'T BURN HER IN THE LEAST! IT'S NO FIRE AT ALL, BUT ONLY A DECEPTION.
INDEED, TO WATCH TH LITTLE QUEEN MARCH CALMLY THROUGH THE FLAMES RESTORED COURAGE TO EVERY MEMBER OF THE PARTY
THIS IS SURELY A MOST EXTRAORDINARY ADVENTURE.
IT UPSETS ALL THE NATURAL LAWS THAT I HEARD PROFESSO NOWITALL TEACH IN THE SCHOOL-HOUSE.

WE'RE NOT EVEN BEING SCORCHED!

THE WALLS OF THE EMERALD CITY ARE PLAINLY VISIBLE, SO I BID YOU GOOD-BYE.

WE'RE VERY GRATEFUL TO YOUR MAJESTY FOR YOUR KIND ASSISTANCE.

I'M ALWAYS PLEASED TO BE OF SERVICE TO MY FRIENDS.

*A*S THE QUEEN DARTED AWAY HOME, THE TRAVELERS APPROACHED THE EMERALD CITY.

I'LL PROD THE FIRST THAT COMES NEAR!

AT THE WORST THEY CAN BUT SCRATCH MY BEAUTIFUL NICKEL-PLATE.

BUT THERE'LL BE NO "WORST," FOR I THINK I CAN FRIGHTEN THESE ABSURD SOLDIERS EASILY.

FOLLOW ME CLOSELY, ALL OF YOU!

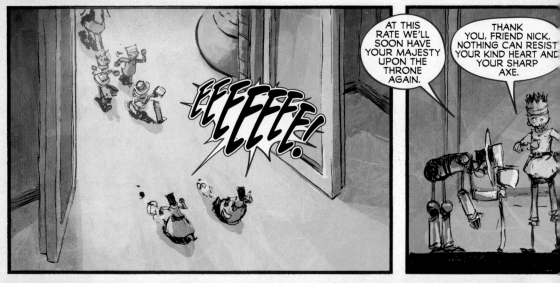

AT THIS RATE WE'LL SOON HAVE YOUR MAJESTY UPON THE THRONE AGAIN.

EEEEEEE!

THANK YOU, FRIEND NICK. NOTHING CAN RESIST YOUR KIND HEART AND YOUR SHARP AXE.

THE TRAVELERS MARCHED TOWARD THE ROYAL PALACE.

WHAT'S HAPPENED?

WE'VE HAD A REVOLUTION, YOUR MAJESTY, AS YOU OUGHT TO KNOW VERY WELL. SINCE YOU WENT AWAY THE WOMEN HAVE BEEN RUNNING THINGS TO SUIT THEMSELVES.

I'M GLAD YOU'VE COME BACK TO RESTORE ORDER. DOIN' HOUSEWORK AND MINDING THE CHILDREN IS WEARING OUT EVERY MAN IN THE EMERALD CITY.

HM. HOW DID THE WOMEN MANAGE IT SO EASILY?

I REALLY DON'T KNOW. PERHAPS THE WOMEN ARE MADE OF CAST-IRON.

*A*S THEY PASSED ALONG THE STREET, NO MOVEMENT WAS MADE TO OPPOSE THEIR PROGRESS.

I'M AFRAID WE'RE WALKING INTO A TRAP.

NON-SENSE! THE SILLY CREATURES ARE CONQUERED ALREADY!

IT'S TOO EASY, ALTOGETHER. LOOK OUT FOR TROUBLE AHEAD.

INTO THE MAGNIFICENT THRONE ROOM MARCHED THE TIN WOODMAN AND HIS FOLLOWERS.

HOW DARE YOU SIT IN MY THRONE? DON'T YOU KNOW YOU'RE GUILTY OF TREASON, AND THAT THERE'S A LAW AGAINST TREASON?

MMMMMMMM...

THE THRONE BELONGS TO WHOEVER IS ABLE TO TAKE IT. I HAVE TAKEN IT, SO JUST NOW *I* AM THE QUEEN.

ALL WHO OPPOSE ME ARE GUILTY OF TREASON, AND MUST BE PUNISHED BY THE LAW YOU'VE JUST MENTIONED.

HOW *IS* THAT, FRIEND NICK?

WHEN IT COMES TO LAW, I'VE NOTHING TO SAY. LAWS WERE NEVER MEANT TO B UNDERSTOOD, AND IT'S FOOLISH TO MAKE THE ATTEMPT.

WHY DON'T OU MARRY THE JEEN? THEN YOU CAN *BOTH* RULE.

WHY DON'T YOU SEND HER BACK TO HER MOTHER, WHERE SHE BELONGS?

WHY DON'T YOU SHUT HER UP IN A CLOSET UNTIL SHE BEHAVES HERSELF, AND PROMISES TO BE GOOD?

OR GIVE HER A GOOD SHAKING!

NO, WE MUST TREAT THE POOR GIRL WITH GENTLENESS. LET'S GIVE HER ALL THE JEWELS SHE CAN CARRY, AND SEND HER AWAY HAPPY AND CONTENTED.

HA HA HA! YOU'RE VERY ABSURD CREATURES!

BUT I'M TIRED OF YOUR NONSENSE AND HAVE NO TIME TO BOTHER WITH YOU LONGER.

HA HA HA!

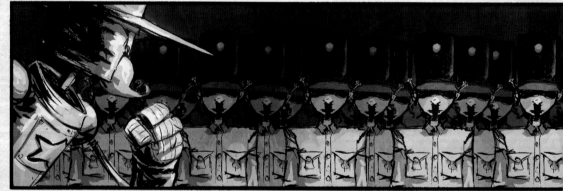

YOU SEE HOW FOOLISH IT IS TO OPPOSE A WOMAN'S WIT! THIS ONLY *PROVES* THAT I'M MORE FIT TO RULE THE EMERALD CITY THAN A SCARE-CROW.

I BEAR YOU NO ILL WILL -- BUT LEST YOU SHOULD PROVE TROUBLESOME TO ME IN THE FUTURE I SHALL ORDER YOU ALL TO BE DESTROYED.

ALL EXCEPT THE BOY, WHO BELONGS TO OLD MOMBI AND MUST BE RESTORED TO HER KEEPING. THE REST OF YOU AREN'T HUMAN, AND THEREFORE IT WON'T BE WICKED TO DEMOLISH YOU.

THE SAW-HORSE AND THE PUMPKIN-HEAD'S BODY I'LL HAVE CHOPPED UP FOR KINDLING-WOOD, AND THE PUMPKIN SHALL BE MADE INTO TARTS.

THE SCARECROW WILL DO NICELY TO START A BONFIRE, AND THE TIN MAN CAN BE CUT INTO SMALL PIECES AND FED TO THE GOATS.

AS FOR THIS IMMENSE WOGGLE-BUG --

HIGHLY MAGNIFIED, IF YOU PLEASE!

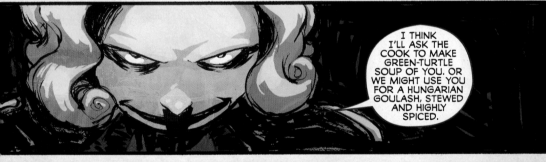

I THINK I'LL ASK THE COOK TO MAKE GREEN-TURTLE SOUP OF YOU. OR WE MIGHT USE YOU FOR A HUNGARIAN GOULASH, STEWED AND HIGHLY SPICED.

I FEAR I'VE WOGGLED MY LAST WIGGLE!

I CAN SEE A FINE CASE OF INDIGESTION AHEAD.

EEEEEEEK!

EEEEEEEEE!

EEEEEEE!

EEEEEEE!

YOWWWWWWWWW...

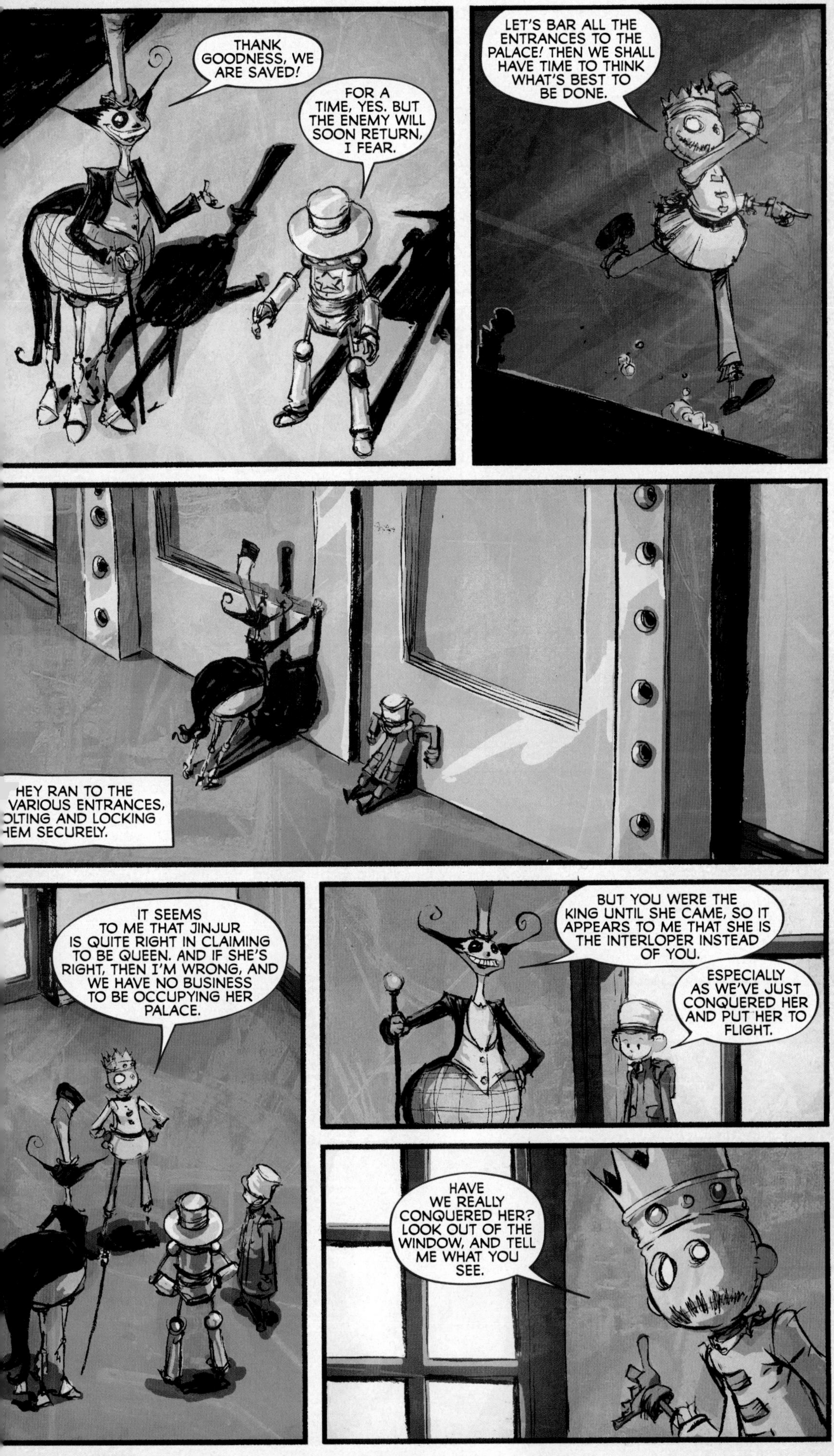
THANK GOODNESS, WE ARE SAVED!
FOR A TIME, YES. BUT THE ENEMY WILL SOON RETURN, I FEAR.
LET'S BAR ALL THE ENTRANCES TO THE PALACE! THEN WE SHALL HAVE TIME TO THINK WHAT'S BEST TO BE DONE.
HEY RAN TO THE VARIOUS ENTRANCES, OLTING AND LOCKING HEM SECURELY.
IT SEEMS TO ME THAT JINJUR IS QUITE RIGHT IN CLAIMING TO BE QUEEN. AND IF SHE'S RIGHT, THEN I'M WRONG, AND WE HAVE NO BUSINESS TO BE OCCUPYING HER PALACE.
BUT YOU WERE THE KING UNTIL SHE CAME, SO IT APPEARS TO ME THAT SHE IS THE INTERLOPER INSTEAD OF YOU.
ESPECIALLY AS WE'VE JUST CONQUERED HER AND PUT HER TO FLIGHT.
HAVE WE REALLY CONQUERED HER? LOOK OUT OF THE WINDOW, AND TELL ME WHAT YOU SEE.

THE PALACE IS SURROUNDED BY A DOUBLE ROW OF GIRL SOLDIERS.

WE'RE AS TRULY THEIR PRISONERS AS WE WERE BEFORE THE MICE FRIGHTENED THEM FROM THE PALACE.

I HOPE JINJUR CANNOT GET AT US! SHE THREATENED TO MAKE TARTS OF ME, YOU KNOW.

DON'T WORRY. IF YOU STAY SHUT UP HERE YOU'D SPOIL IN TIME, ANYWAY. AND A GOOD TART IS FAR MORE ADMIRABLE THAN A DECAYED INTELLECT.

YOU'D BELONG TO THE UPPER CRUST THEN.

WHY, DEAR FATHER, DIDN'T YOU MAKE ME OUT OF TIN -- OR EVEN OUT OF STRAW?

SHUCKS! YOU OUGHT TO BE GLAD THAT I MADE YOU AT ALL.

THIS TERRIBLE QUEEN JINJUR SUGGESTED MAKING A GOULASH OF ME -- ME! THE ONLY HIGHLY MAGNIFIED AND THOROUGHLY EDUCATED WOGGLE-BUG IN THE WIDE, WIDE WORLD!

DON'T YOU IMAGINE HE'D MAKE A BETTER SOUP?

A BRILLIANT IDEA.

I CAN SEE, IN MY MIND'S EYE, THE GOATS EATING SMALL PIECES OF MY DEAR COMRADE, THE TIN WOOD-MAN...

...WHILE MY SOUP IS BEING COOKED ON A BON-FIRE BUILT OF THE SAW-HORSE AND JACK PUMPKINHEAD'S BODY...

...AND QUEEN JINJUR WATCHES ME BOIL WHILE SHE FEEDS THE FLAMES WITH MY FRIEND THE SCARECROW!

IT CAN'T HAPPEN FOR SOME TIME, FOR WE SHALL BE ABLE TO KEEP JINJUR OUT OF THE PALACE UNTIL SHE MANAGES TO BREAK DOWN THE DOORS.

IN THE MEANTIME I'M LIABLE TO STARVE TO DEATH.

I THINK THAT I COULD LIVE FOR SOME TIME ON JACK PUMPKIN-HEAD. NOT THAT I PREFER PUMPKINS FOR FOOD --

HOW *HEARTLESS!*

LET'S END THIS MOURNFUL TALK AND TRY TO DISCOVER A MEANS TO ESCAPE.

I BELIEVE I'LL THINK FOR A FEW MINUTES, SO I'LL THANK YOU, TIP, TO GET OUT YOUR KNIFE AND RIP THIS HEAVY CROWN FROM MY FOREHEAD.

OOPS!

WHAT'S THIS?

BE CAREFUL! THAT'S MY POWDER OF LIFE. DON'T SPILL IT, FOR IT'S NEARLY GONE.

WHAT IS THE POWDER OF LIFE?

IT'S SOME MAGICAL STUFF OLD MOMBI GOT FROM A CROOKED SORCERER. SHE BROUGHT JACK TO LIFE WITH IT, AND AFTERWARD I USED IT TO BRING THE SAW-HORSE TO LIFE.

I GUESS IT'LL MAKE ANYTHING LIVE THAT'S SPRINKLED WITH IT, BUT THERE'S ONLY ABOUT ONE DOSE LEFT.

THEN IT'S VERY PRECIOUS.

THAT'S MY LAST MEMENTO OF ROYALTY, AND I'M GLAD TO GET RID OF IT. THE FORMER KING OF THIS CITY, WHO WAS NAMED PASTORIA, LOST THE CROWN TO THE WONDERFUL WIZARD, WHO PASSED IT ON TO ME.

NOW JINJUR CLAIMS IT, AND I SINCERELY HOPE IT WILL NOT GIVE HER A HEAD-ACHE.

AND NOW I'LL INDULGE IN A QUIET THINK.

*T*HE OTHERS REMAINED AS SILENT AS POSSIBLE, SO AS NOT TO DISTURB HIM.

AFTER WHAT SEEMED A VERY LONG TIME INDEED --

MY BRAINS WORK BEAUTIFULLY TODAY!

LISTEN! IF WE ATTEMPT TO ESCAPE THROUGH THE DOORS OF THE PALACE WE SHALL SURELY BE CAPTURED. AND, AS WE CAN'T ESCAPE THROUGH THE GROUND, THERE'S ONLY ONE OTHER THING TO BE DONE.

WE MUST ESCAPE THROUGH THE AIR! ANY SORT OF THING THAT CAN FLY CAN CARRY US EASILY!

I SUGGEST THAT THE TIN WOODMAN SHALL BUILD SOME SORT OF A FLYING MACHINE, WITH GOOD STRONG WINGS.

TIP CAN THEN BRING THE THING TO LIFE WITH HIS MAGICAL POWDER.

BRAVO!

WHAT SPLENDID BRAINS!

REALLY QUITE CLEVER!

I BELIEVE IT CAN BE DONE...IF THE TIN WOODMAN IS EQUAL TO MAKING THE THING.

I DON'T OFTEN FAIL IN WHAT I ATTEMPT. BUT THE THING WILL HAVE TO BE BUILT ON THE ROOF OF THE PALACE, SO IT CAN RISE COMFORTABLY INTO THE AIR.

TO BE SURE!

LET'S SEARCH THROUGH THE PALACE AND CARRY ALL THE MATERIAL WE CAN FIND TO THE ROOF.

FIRST, I BEG YOU'LL MAKE ME ANOTHER LEG TO WALK WITH. IN MY PRESENT CONDITION I'M OF NO USE.

So THE TIN WOODMAN KNOCKED A MAHOGANY CENTER-TABLE TO PIECES WITH HIS AXE.

IT SEEMS STRANGE THAT MY LEFT LEG SHOULD BE THE MOST ELEGANT AND SUBSTANTIAL PART OF ME.

THAT PROVES YOU'RE UNUSUAL. I'M CONVINCED THAT THE ONLY PEOPLE WORTHY OF CONSIDERATION ARE THE UNUSUAL ONES. COMMON FOLKS ARE LIKE THE LEAVES OF A TREE, AND LIVE AND DIE UNNOTICED.

SPOKEN LIKE A PHILOSOPHER!

AS GOOD AS NEW.

THEN LET'S GET TO WORK AND SEE WHAT WE CAN FIND THAT'LL FLY.

THE FRIENDS REASSEMBLED UPON THE ROOF WITH A REMARKABLE ASSORTMENT OF ARTICLES.

I'VE TAKEN FROM ITS POSITION OVER THE MANTELPIECE IN THE GREAT HALLWAY THIS HEAD OF A GUMP.

WE -- HUFF -- BROUGHT A SOFA--HUFF HUFF...

I BROUGHT THE FIRST THING I SAW.

SOMEHOW I'VE BECOME A BIT ENTANGLED...

I'VE BEEN TO THE COUR YARD AND CU LEAVES FROM HUGE PALM TREE.

MY DEAR NICK! YOU'RE GUILTY OF THE GREATEST CRIME ANY PERSON CAN COMMIT IN THE EMERALD CITY!

THE PENALTY FOR CHOPPING LEAVES FROM THE ROYAL PALM IS TO BE KILLED SEVEN TIMES AND AFTERWARD IMPRISONED FOR LIFE.

ONE MORE REASON WHY IT'S NECESSARY FOR US TO ESCAPE.

IF NICK CAN MANUFACTURE -- FROM THIS MESS OF RUBBISH -- A THING THAT WILL CARRY US TO SAFETY, THEN I'LL ACKNOWLEDGE HIM TO BE A BETTER MECHANIC THAN I SUSPECTED.

THE FIRST THING REQUIRED IS A BODY BIG ENOUGH TO CARRY THE ENTIRE PARTY.

THIS SOFA MIGHT BE USED FOR A BODY, BUT SHOULD THE MACHINE EVER TIP SIDEWAYS, WE'D ALL SLIDE OFF.

WHY NOT USE TWO SOFAS? THERE'S ANOTHER ONE JUST LIKE THIS DOWNSTAIRS.

THAT'S A VERY SENSIBLE SUGGESTION.

TIP AND THE SAW-HORSE MANAGED TO GET THE SECOND SOFA TO THE ROOF.

EXCELLENT! WE CAN RIDE WITHIN THIS SNUG NEST QUITE AT OUR EASE.

THIS WILL SHOW WHICH IS THE FRONT END OF THE THING. AND, REALLY, THE GUMP LOOKS VERY WELL AS A FIGURE-HEAD.

THESE GREAT PALM LEAVES -- FOR WHICH I'VE ENDANGERED MY LIFE SEVEN TIMES -- MUST SERVE US AS WINGS.

ARE THEY STRONG ENOUGH?

THEY'RE AS STRONG AS ANYTHING WE CAN GET. ALTHOUGH THEY'RE NOT IN PROPORTION TO THE THING'S BODY, WE'RE NOT IN A POSITION TO BE VERY PARTICULAR.

THE THING IS NOW COMPLETE, AND ONLY NEEDS TO BE BROUGHT TO LIFE.

AREN'T YOU GOING TO USE MY BROOM?

WHAT FOR?

FOR A *TAIL!* SURELY YOU WOULDN'T CALL THE THING COMPLETE WITH-OUT A TAIL!

HM! I DON'T SEE THE USE OF A TAIL. WE'RE NOT TRYING TO COPY A BEAST OR A FISH OR A BIRD. ALL W ASK OF THE THING IS TO CARRY US THROUGH THE AIR.

PERHAPS IT CAN USE A TAIL TO STEER WITH. IF IT FLIES THROUGH THE AIR IT WON'T BE UNLIKE A BIRD. AND ALL BIRDS HAVE TAILS, WHICH THEY USE FOR A RUDDER WHILE FLYING.

VERY WELL -- THE BROOM SHALL BE USED FOR A TAIL. NOW, TIP, BRING IT TO LIFE.

THE THING LOOKS VERY BIG. I'M NOT SURE THERE'S ENOUGH POWDER LEFT, BUT I'LL MAKE IT GO AS FAR AS POSSIBLE.

PUT MOST ON THE WINGS, FOR THEY MUST BE MADE STRONG.

AND DON'T FORGET THE HEAD!

OR THE TAIL!

DO BE QUIET. YOU MUST GIVE ME THE CHANCE TO WORK THE MAGIC CHARM IN THE PROPER MANNER.

THE HEAD! *THE HEAD!* DON'T, I BEG OF YOU, FORGET THE HEAD!

THERE'S ONLY A LITTLE OF THE POWDER LEFT. SEEMS TO ME IT'S MORE IMPORTANT TO BRING THE LEGS TO LIFE THAN THE HEAD.

NOT SO. EVERYTHING MUST HAVE A HEAD TO DIRECT IT.

SINCE THIS CREATURE IS TO FLY AND NOT WALK, IT'S UNIMPORTANT WHETHER ITS LEGS ARE ALIVE OR NOT.

NOW, KEEP SILENCE WHILE I WORK THE CHARM.

WEAUGH!

TEAUGH!

PEAUGH!

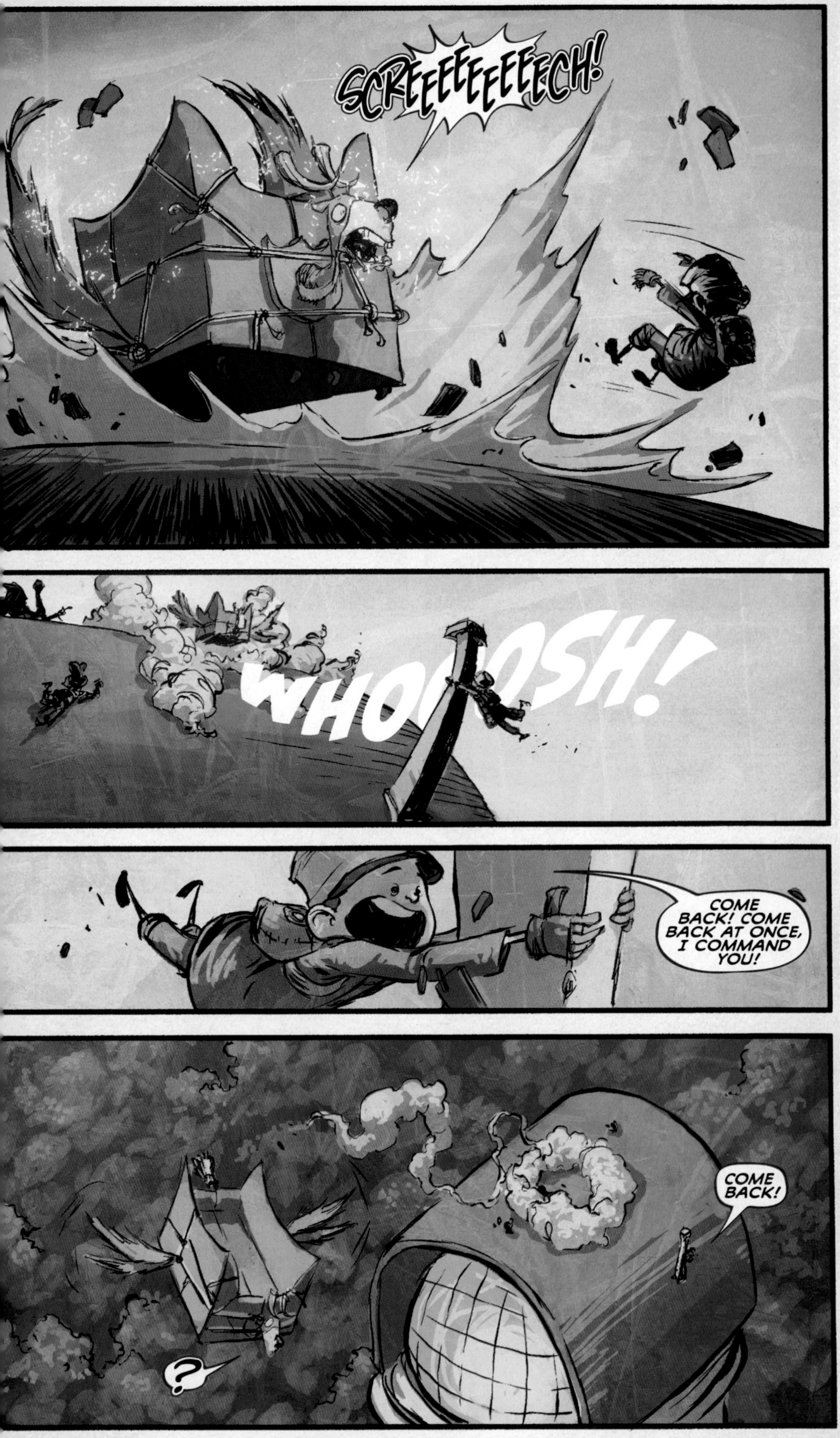
SCREEEEEEEEECH!
WHOOOOSH!
COME BACK! COME BACK AT ONCE, I COMMAND YOU!
COME BACK!
?

THIS IS THE MOST NOVEL EXPERIENCE I EVER HEARD OF.

THE LAST THING I REMEMBER IS WALKING THROUG THE FOREST AND HEARING A LOUD NOISE.

SOME-ONE PROBABLY KILLED ME THEN. YET HERE I AM, ALIVE AGAIN...

...WITH A BODY WHICH WOULD MAKE ANY RESPECTABLE ANIMAL WEEP WITH SHAME.

WHAT DOES IT ALL MEAN? AM I A GUMP OR AM I A JUGGER-NAUT?

YOU'RE JUST A THING WITH A GUMP'S HEAD. WE'VE BROUGHT YOU TO LIFE TO CARRY US THROUGH THE AIR.

AS I'M NOT A GUMP, I MAY AS WELL BECOME YOUR SERVANT AS ANYTHING ELSE.

MY ONLY SATISFACTION IS THAT I DON'T SEEM TO HAVE A VERY STRONG CONSTITUTION AND AM NOT LIKELY TO LIVE LONG IN A STATE OF SLAVERY.

ARE YOU NOT FEELING WELL TODAY?

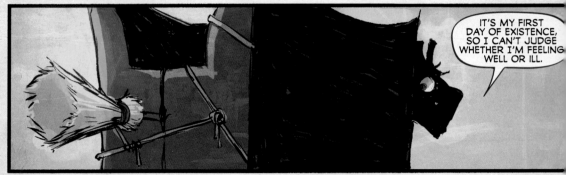

IT'S MY FIRST DAY OF EXISTENCE, SO I CAN'T JUDGE WHETHER I'M FEELING WELL OR ILL.

ME, COME! DO TRY TO BE E CHEERFUL. WE SHALL BE MASTERS AND STRIVE TO NDER YOUR EXISTENCE AS PLEASANT AS POSSIBLE.

ARE YOU WILLING TO CARRY US THROUGH THE AIR WHEREVER WE WISH TO GO?

CERTAINLY! I GREATLY PREFER TO NAVIGATE THE AIR.

FOR SHOULD I TRAVEL ON THE EARTH AND MEET WITH ONE OF MY OWN SPECIES, MY EMBARRASSMENT WOULD BE SOMETHING AWFUL!

AND YET, MY MASTERS, NONE OF YOU SEEMS TO BE CONSTRUCTED MUCH MORE ARTISTICALLY THAN I AM.

PPEARANCES E DECEITFUL. I M BOTH HIGHLY AGNIFIED AND THOROUGHLY EDUCATED.

INDEED!

MY BRAINS ARE CONSIDERED REMARKABLY RARE SPECIMENS.

HOW STRANGE!

I OWN A HEART ALTOGETHER THE WARMEST AND MOST ADMIRABLE IN THE WHOLE WORLD.

I'M DELIGHTED TO HEAR IT. KOFF-KOFF

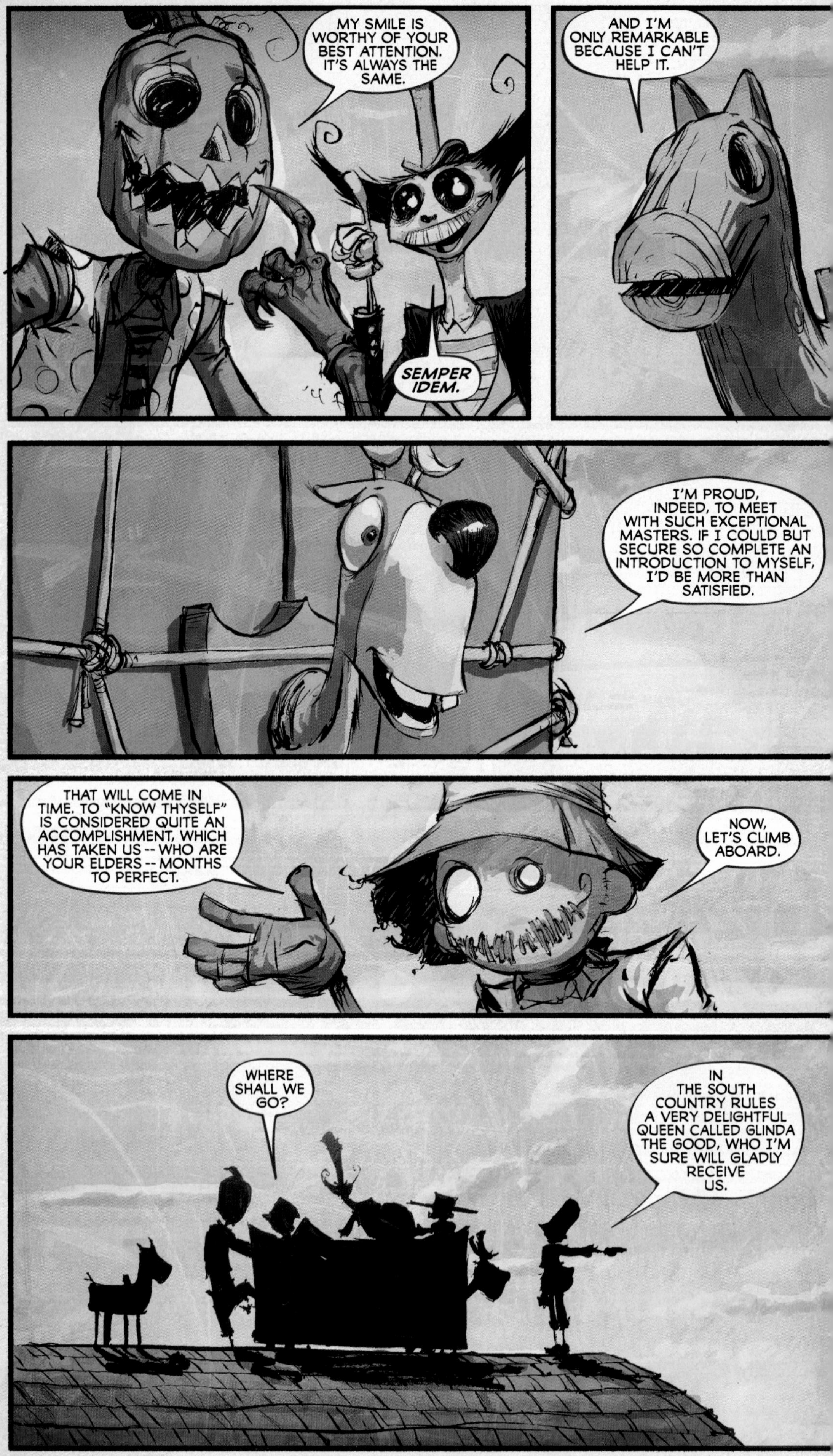
MY SMILE IS WORTHY OF YOUR BEST ATTENTION. IT'S ALWAYS THE SAME.
SEMPER IDEM.
AND I'M ONLY REMARKABLE BECAUSE I CAN'T HELP IT.
I'M PROUD, INDEED, TO MEET WITH SUCH EXCEPTIONAL MASTERS. IF I COULD BUT SECURE SO COMPLETE AN INTRODUCTION TO MYSELF, I'D BE MORE THAN SATISFIED.
THAT WILL COME IN TIME. TO "KNOW THYSELF" IS CONSIDERED QUITE AN ACCOMPLISHMENT, WHICH HAS TAKEN US -- WHO ARE YOUR ELDERS -- MONTHS TO PERFECT.
NOW, LET'S CLIMB ABOARD.
WHERE SHALL WE GO?
IN THE SOUTH COUNTRY RULES A VERY DELIGHTFUL QUEEN CALLED GLINDA THE GOOD, WHO I'M SURE WILL GLADLY RECEIVE US.

LET'S GO TO HER AND ASK HER ADVICE.

I BELIEVE SHE'LL PROVE A FRIEND INDEED.

ARE WE ALL READY?

YES.

THEN BE KIND ENOUGH TO FLY SOUTHWARD -- AND DON'T GO HIGHER THAN TO ESCAPE THE HOUSES AND TREES, FOR IT MAKES ME DIZZY TO BE UP SO FAR.

ALL RIGHT.

FLOP FLOP FLOP FLOP FLOP FLOP

WE'RE OFF!

THE SCENIC EFFECT FROM THIS ALTITUDE IS MARVELOUS.

NEVER MIND THE SCENERY! HOLD ON TIGHT, OR YOU MAY GET A TUMBLE. THE THING SEEMS TO ROCK BADLY.

PERHAPS WE SHOULD HAVE WAITED UNTIL MORNING. I WONDER IF THE GUMP CAN FLY IN THE NIGHT.

I'VE BEEN WONDERING THAT MYSELF.

THIS IS A NEW EXPERIENCE. I USED TO HAVE LEGS THAT CARRIED ME OVER THE GROUND. BUT NOW MY LEGS FEEL AS IF THEY WERE ASLEEP.

THEY ARE -- WE DIDN'T BRING 'EM TO LIFE.

YOU'RE EXPECTED TO FLY, NOT TO WALK.

WE CAN WALK OUR SELVES.

WONDER IF RIDING
ROUGH THE AIR IS
LIABLE TO SPOIL
PUMPKINS.

NOT UNLESS
YOU DROP YOUR
HEAD OVER THE
SIDE.

IN THAT
EVENT YOUR
HEAD WOULD NO
LONGER BE A
PUMPKIN, FOR IT
WOULD BECOME
A SQUASH.

HAVEN'T WE
ASKED YOU TO
RESTRAIN THESE
UNFEELING
JOKES?

YOU
HAVE, AND
I'VE RESTRAINED
A GOOD MANY
OF THEM.

BUT THERE ARE OPPORTUNITIES
FOR *SO MANY* EXCELLENT PUNS IN
OUR LANGUAGE. TO AN EDUCATED
PERSON LIKE MYSELF, THE TEMPTATION
TO EXPRESS THEM IS ALMOST
IRRESISTIBLE.

PEOPLE WITH
MORE OR LESS
EDUCATION
DISCOVERED
THOSE PUNS
CENTURIES
AGO.

ARE YOU
SURE?

HROW IT OVERBOARD.
T'S QUITE EMPTY NOW.
THERE'S NO USE
KEEPING IT.

IS
IT REALLY
EMPTY?

OF
COURSE. I
SHOOK OUT
EVERY GRAIN
OF THE
POWDER.

BUT THE BOTTOM
ON THE INSIDE IS FULLY
AN INCH AWAY FROM
THE BOTTOM ON THE
OUTSIDE.

LET ME
SEE.

YES, THE THING CERTAINLY HAS A FALSE BOTTOM.

MY FINGERS ARE RATHER STIFF-- PLEASE SEE IF YOU CAN OPEN IT.

*T*IP HAD NO DIFFICULTY IN UNSCREWING THE BOTTOM.

"DR. NIKIDIK'S CELEBRATED WISHING PILLS.

"DIRECTIONS FOR USE: SWALLOW ONE PILL, COUNT SEVENTEEN BY TWOS, THEN MAKE A WISH. THE WISH WILL IMMEDIATELY BE GRANTED.

"CAUTION: KEEP IN A DRY AND DARK PLACE."

WHY, THIS IS A VERY VALUABLE DISCOVERY! THESE PILLS MAY BE OF GREAT USE.

I WONDER IF OLD MOMBI KNEW THEY WERE IN THE BOTTOM OF THE PEPPERBOX. I REMEMBER HEARING HER SAY SHE GOT THE POWDER OF LIFE FROM THIS SAME NIKIDIK.

HE MUST BE A POWERFUL SORCERER! SINCE THE POWDER PROVED A SUCCESS WE OUGHT TO HAVE CONFIDENCE IN THE PILLS.

BUT HOW CAN ANYONE COUNT SEVENTEEN BY TWOS? SEVENTEEN IS AN ODD NUMBER.

THEN THE PILLS ARE OF NO USE TO US -- THIS FACT OVERWHELMS ME WITH GRIEF. FOR I'D INTENDED WISHING THAT MY HEAD WOULD NEVER SPOIL.

NONSENSE! WE'D MAKE FAR BETTER WISHES THAN THAT.

IF YOU WERE LIABLE TO SPOIL AT ANY TIME YOU COULD UNDER-STAND MY ANXIETY.

I SYMPATHIZE WITH YOU. BUT SINCE NO ONE CAN POSSIBLY COUNT SEVENTEEN BY TWOS, SYMPATHY IS ALL YOU'RE LIABLE TO GET.

THE GUMP FLEW ON, AND FOR SOME REASON ROCKED MORE AND MORE DIZZILY EVERY HOUR.

THE WOGGLE-BUG DECLARED HE WAS SEASICK AND TIP WAS ALSO SOMEWHAT DISTRESSED. BUT THE OTHERS DIDN'T SEEM TO MIND THE MOTION.

HOW ARE WE TO KNOW WHEN WE COME TO THE PALACE OF GLINDA THE GOOD? WE CAN'T SEE A SINGLE THING DOWN ON THE EARTH.

I DON'T SEE HOW WE CAN STOP JUST NOW.

WE MIGHT ALIGHT IN A RIVER OR ON THE TOP OF A STEEPLE, AND THAT WOULD BE A DISASTER.

So THEY PERMITTED THE GUMP TO FLY ON AND WAITED PATIENTLY FOR MORNING.

TIP'S FEARS WERE PROVEN TO BE WELL FOUNDED.

WE'RE LOST!

THE GUMP MUST HAVE CARRIED US OUT OF THE LAND OF OZ AND OVER THE DESERT AND INTO THE TERRIBLE OUT- SIDE WORLD THAT DOROTHY TOLD US ABOUT.

WE MUST GET BACK AS SOON AS POSSIBLE!

TURN AROUND!

IF I DO, I SHALL UPSET. I'M NOT USED TO FLYING.

THE BEST PLAN WOULD BE FOR ME TO ALIGHT. THEN I CAN TURN AROUND AND TAKE A FRESH START.

JUST THEN, HOWEVER, THERE SEEMED TO BE NO STOPPING-PLACE.

THEY CAME TO A RANGE OF HIGH MOUNTAINS.

STOP AT THE FIRST LEVEL PLACE YOU SEE!

VERY WELL.

SKKKKRR--

CHONK

PLOP! FLUMP! KONK!

THIS IS A WORSE PRISON THAN THE PALACE.

HOW WE'RE EVER TO ESCAPE FROM THIS JACK-DAWS' NEST I MUST LEAVE TO SOMEONE WITH BETTER BRAINS THAN I POSSESS.

OUR JOURNEY HAS ENDED RATHER SUDDENLY. WE CAN'T JUSTLY BLAME THE GUMP -- HE DID THE BEST HE COULD UNDER THE CIRCUMSTANCES.

I'M AFRAID MOUNTAIN AIR ISN'T GOOD FOR PUMPKINS.

IT WON'T BE WHEN THE JACKDAWS COME BACK. JACKDAWS ARE ESPECIALLY FOND OF PUMPKINS.

DO YOU THINK THE BIRDS WILL COME HERE?

OF COURSE THEY WILL -- THIS IS THEIR NEST. THERE MUST BE HUNDREDS OF THEM -- SEE WHAT A LOT OF THINGS THEY'VE BROUGHT HERE!

LOOK AT WHAT I'VE TURNED UP AMONG THE RUBBISH -- A BEAUTIFUL DIAMOND NECKLACE!

*T*HIS NECKLACE WAS SO GREATLY ADMIRED BY THE TIN WOODMAN THAT THE WOGGLE-BUG PRESENTED IT TO HIM WITH A GRACEFUL SPEECH.

THE JACKDAWS ARE COMING! IF THEY FIND US HERE THEY'LL SURELY KILL US IN THEIR ANGER!

MY TIME HAS COME!

MINE, ALSO! JACKDAWS ARE THE GREATEST ENEMY OF MY RACE!

THE SCARECROW COMMANDED TIP TO TAKE OFF JACK'S HEAD AND LIE DOWN BESIDE THE WOGGLE-BUG.

Caw
Caw
Caw

NICK CHOPPER SCATTERED THE SCARECROW'S STRAW, COMPLETELY COVERING THEIR BODIES.

Caw
Caw
Caw

Caw
Caw-Awk!
Caw

Rawk-Awk!
Caw

Caw
Caw
Caw

THEY'RE DROPPING MY STRAW INTO THE GULF! SAVE ME, NICK! STOP THIS WANTON DESTRUCTION OF MY INTERIOR!

...WHICH FILLED THE BIRDS WITH TERROR.

GOOD THING MY EYES ARE OF GLASS AND CAN'T BE INJURED.

caw

*T*HE GUMP BEGAN FLOPPING ITS REMAINING WINGS...

caw

caw

AS THEY FLED, THE GUMP'S EXERTIONS FREED IT FROM THE ROCK.

WE'RE SAVED!

WE ARE, INDEED!

WE OWE IT ALL TO THE FLOPPING OF THE THING AND THE GOOD AXE OF THE WOODMAN!

JACK!

IF I'M SAVED, GET ME OUT OF HERE!

TIP PLACED THE PUMPKIN UPON ITS NECK AGAIN AND SET THE SAW-HORSE UPRIGHT.

WE OWE YOU MANY THANKS FOR THE GALLANT FIGHT YOU MADE.

I REALLY THINK WE'VE ESCAPED VERY NICELY.

NOT SO!

I'M COMPLETELY RUINED! WHERE IS THE STRAW THAT STUFFS MY BODY? THE JACKDAWS FLUNG IT ALL INTO THE CHASM!

MY POOR FRIEND! WHOEVER COULD IMAGINE YOU'D COME TO THIS UNTIMELY END?

I DID IT TO SAVE MY FRIENDS. I'M GLAD I PERISHED IN SO NOBLE AND UNSELFISH A MANNER.

THE SCARECROW'S CLOTHING IS STILL SAFE.

WHY NOT STUFF HIM WITH MONEY?

MONEY!

IN THE NEST ARE THOUSANDS OF DOLLAR BILLS -- AND TWO-DOLLAR BILLS -- AND FIVE-DOLLAR BILLS -- AND TENS AND TWENTIES AND FIFTIES.

ENOUGH TO STUFF A *DOZEN* SCARE-CROWS.

WHAT WE'D THOUGHT ONLY WORTHLESS PAPERS ARE BILLS!

THERE'S AN IMMENSE FORTUNE IN THIS INACCESSIBLE NEST.

SO THE SCARECROW'S LEFT LEG WAS STUFFED WITH FIVE-DOLLAR BILLS, AND HIS RIGHT LEG STUFFED WITH TEN-DOLLAR BILLS.

MY BODY IS SO CLOSELY FILLED WITH FIFTIES, ONE-HUNDREDS, AND ONE-THOUSANDS, I CAN SCARCELY CLOSE MY JACKET.

YOU'RE NOW THE MOST VALUABLE MEMBER OF OUR PARTY.

YOU'RE MADE OF MONEY.

I BEG YOU TO REMEMBER THAT MY BRAINS ARE STILL COMPOSED OF THE SAME OLD MATERIAL. AND THEY'VE ALWAYS MADE ME A PERSON TO BE DEPENDED ON IN AN EMERGENCY.

WELL, THE EMERGENCY IS HERE. UNLESS YOUR BRAINS HELP US OUT WE'LL BE COMPELLED TO PASS THE REMAINDER OF OUR LIVES IN THIS NEST.

HOW ABOUT THESE WISHING PILLS? CAN'T WE USE THEM TO ESCAPE?

NOT UNLESS WE CAN COUNT SEVENTEEN BY TWOS.

THE PROFESSOR CLAIMED ANYTHING COULD BE DONE WITH X'S AND Y'S AND A'S AND SUCH THINGS, BY MIXING THEM UP WITH PLENTY OF PLUSSES AND MINUSES AND EQUALS, AND SO FORTH.

STOP! STOP! YOU'RE MAKING MY HEAD ACHE!

YOUR MATHEMATICS SEEM LIKE A BOTTLE OF MIXED PICKLES -- THE MORE YOU FISH FOR WHAT YOU WANT, THE LESS CHANCE YOU HAVE OF GETTING IT.

WHY NOT START COUNTING AT A HALF OF ONE? THEN ANYONE CAN COUNT UP TO SEVENTEEN BY TWOS VERY EASILY.

YOU MAKE ME QUITE ASHAMED OF MYSELF.

THE SAW-HORSE IS RIGHT.

TWICE ONE-HALF IS ONE, AND IF YOU GET TO ONE, IT'S EASY TO COUNT UP TO SEVENTEEN BY TWOS.

I WONDER DIDN'T THINK OF THAT MY-SELF.

LET'S MAKE A WISH AT ONCE. WHO'LL SWALLOW THE FIRST PILL?

SUPPOSE YOU DO IT?

I CAN'T-- MY MOUTH IS PAINTED ON, AND THERE'S NO SWALLOW CONNECTED WITH IT.

IN FACT, I BELIEVE TIP AND THE WOGGLE-BUG ARE THE ONLY ONES ABLE TO SWALLOW.

THEN I'LL MAKE THE FIRST WISH. GIVE ME ONE OF THE PILLS.

COUNT!

ONE-HALF, ONE, THREE, FIVE, SEVEN, NINE, ELEVEN, THIRTEEN, FIFTEEN, SEVENTEEN!

OHHH! OOOOO! THE PILL HAS POISONED ME! OUCH! MURDER! FIRE!

WHAT CAN WE DO FOR YOU? SPEAK, I BEG!

OOH! I -- I DON'T KNOW! OHHH! I WISH I'D NEVER SWALLOWED THAT PILL!

WHAT'S HAPPENED?

WHY, THE THREE PILLS ARE IN THE BOX AGAIN!

OF COURSE. DIDN'T TIP WISH THAT HE'D NEVER SWALLOWED ONE OF THEM?

WELL, THE WISH CAME TRUE AND HE DIDN'T SWALLOW ONE OF THEM. SO THEY ARE ALL THREE IN THE BOX.

THAT MAY BE, BUT THE PILL GAVE ME A DREADFUL PAIN, JUST THE SAME.

IMPOSSIBLE! IF YOU'VE NEVER SWALLOWED IT, THE PILL CAN'T HAVE GIVEN YOU A PAIN.

THEN IT WAS A SPLENDID IMITATION! YOU TRY THE NEXT PILL YOURSELF. WE'VE WASTED ONE WISH ALREADY.

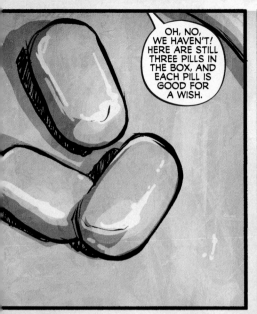

OH, NO, WE HAVEN'T! HERE ARE STILL THREE PILLS IN THE BOX, AND EACH PILL IS GOOD FOR A WISH.

NOW YOU'RE MAKING *MY* HEAD ACHE.

IT REMAINS FOR ME TO SAVE US IN MY MOST HIGHLY MAGNIFIED AND THOROUGHLY EDUCATED MANNER.

THE INSECT COUNTED SEVENTEEN BY TWOS, AND -- PERHAPS BECAUSE OGGLE-BUGS HAVE STRONGER STOMACHS THAN BOYS -- THE SILVER BULLET CAUSED NO PAIN.

I WISH THE GUMP'S BROKEN WINGS MENDED AND AS GOOD AS NEW!

HOORAY!

WE CAN LEAVE THIS MISERABLE NEST WHENEVER WE PLEASE.

IT'S NEARLY DARK. I DON'T LIKE THESE NIGHT TRIPS, FOR ONE NEVER KNOWS WHAT WILL HAPPEN.

IT WAS DECIDED TO WAIT UNTIL DAYLIGHT. THE ADVENTURERS AMUSED THEMSELVES BY SEARCHING THE NEST FOR TREASURES.

THIS NEST WOULD BE A PICNIC FOR JINJUR. AS NEARLY AS I CAN MAKE OUT SHE CONQUERED ME MERELY TO ROB MY CITY OF ITS EMERALDS.

*T*IP ATTACHED A LORGNETTE TO THE NECK OF THE SAW-HORSE.

IT'S VERY PRETTY, BUT WHAT IS IT FOR?

NONE OF THEM COULD ANSWER THAT QUESTION, SO THE SAW-HOR[S]E DECIDED IT WAS SOME RARE DECORATION AND BECAME VERY FOND OF IT.

NEXT MORNING.

THE JACKDAWS!

GUMP, START AT ONCE!

CAW CAW CAW CAW AW[H]

IN A FEW MOMENTS THE[Y] WERE FAR FROM THE NES[T]

AFTER PASSING CITIES AND VILLAGES THE GUMP CARRIED THEM HIGH ABOVE THE DESERT SEPARATING THE REST OF THE WORLD FROM THE LAND OF OZ.

BEFORE NOON THEY WERE ONCE MORE WITHIN THE BORDERS OF THEIR NATIVE LAND.

WE'RE IN THE LAND OF THE MUNCHKINS -- A LONG DISTANCE FROM GLINDA THE GOOD.

THEN THE WOGGLE-BUG MUST SWALLOW ANOTHER PILL AND WISH US HEADED IN THE RIGHT DIRECTION.

BUT THE BOX CONTAINING THE WISHING PILLS WAS NOT TO BE FOUND.

I MUST HAVE LEFT IT IN THE JACKDAWS' NEST. I DESERVE A GOOD SCOLDING FOR MY CARELESSNESS.

THE GUMP FLEW STEADILY ON, CARRYING THEM THEY KNEW NOT WHERE.

WE MUST HAVE REACHED THE SOUTH COUNTRY, FOR EVERY-THING IS RED!

THEN WE'RE WITHIN THE DOMAIN OF GLINDA THE GOOD.

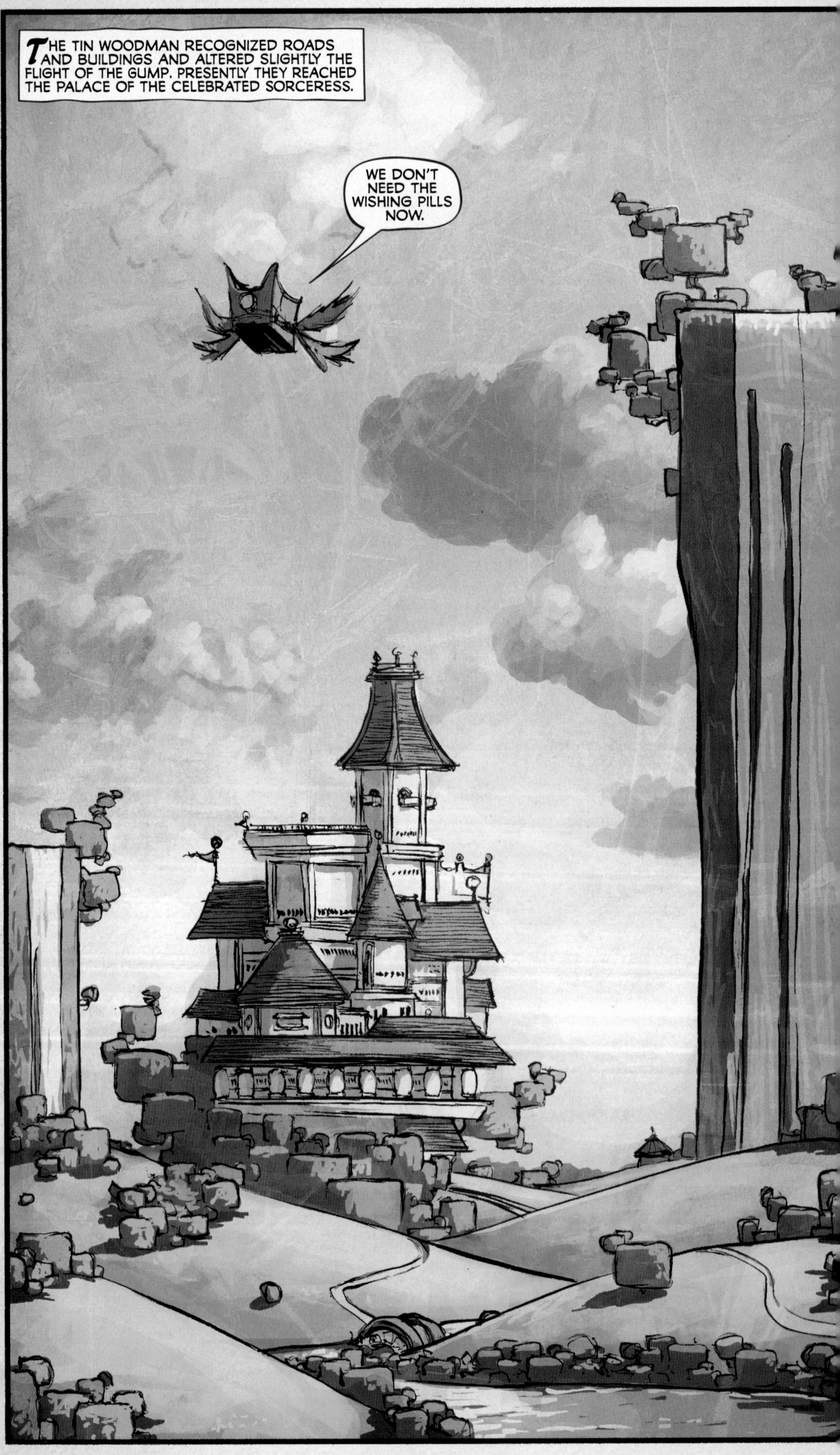
THE TIN WOODMAN RECOGNIZED ROADS AND BUILDINGS AND ALTERED SLIGHTLY THE FLIGHT OF THE GUMP. PRESENTLY THEY REACHED THE PALACE OF THE CELEBRATED SORCERESS.
WE DON'T NEED THE WISHING PILLS NOW.

THAT'S STRANGE!

NOT AT ALL -- GLINDA THE GOOD IS A MIGHTY SORCERESS. I SUPPOSE SHE KNOWS WHY WE CAME AS WELL AS WE DO OURSELVES.

GOOD DAY! WE'VE COME TO REQUEST AN AUDIENCE WITH YOUR FAIR RULER.

GLINDA IS WITHIN HER PALACE, AWAITING YOU. SHE SAW YOU COMING LONG BEFORE YOU ARRIVED.

THEN WHAT WAS THE USE OF OUR COMING?

TO PROVE YOU ARE A PUMPKIN-HEAD!

IF THE SORCERESS EXPECTS US, WE MUST NOT KEEP HER WAITING.

HAIL, BEAUTIFUL QUEEN.

LONG MAY YOU REIGN.

MAY YOU ALSO SNOW AND BLIZZARD.

WHY DO YOU SEEK ME?

I BEG TO ANNOUNCE THAT MY EMERALD CITY HAS BEEN OVERRUN BY A CROWD OF IMPUDENT GIRLS WITH KNITTING-NEEDLES.

THEY'VE ENSLAVED ALL THE MEN, ROBBED THE STREETS AND PUBLIC BUILDING OF ALL THEIR JEWELS, AND USURPED MY THRONE.

I KNOW IT.

THEY ALSO THREATENED TO DESTROY ME, AS WELL AS THE GOOD FRIENDS YOU SEE BEFORE YOU.

HAD WE NOT MANAGED TO ESCAPE THEIR CLUTCHES OUR DAYS WOULD LONG SINCE HAVE ENDED.

I KNOW IT.

THEREFORE I'VE COME TO BEG YOUR ASSISTANCE, FOR I BELIEVE YOU'RE ALWAYS GLAD TO SUCCOR THE UNFORTUNATE AND OPPRESSED.

THAT IS TRUE. BUT THE EMERALD CITY IS NOW RULED BY GENERAL JINJUR, WHO HAS CAUSED HERSELF TO BE PROCLAIMED QUEEN.

WHAT RIGHT HAVE I TO OPPOSE HER?

WHY, SHE STOLE THE THRONE FROM ME.

AND HOW CAME YOU TO POSSESS THE THRONE?

I -- UH -- GOT IT FROM THE WIZARD OF OZ, AND BY THE CHOICE OF THE PEOPLE,

AND WHERE DID THE WIZARD GET IT?

WELL...THAT IS -- I'M TOLD HE TOOK IT FROM PASTORIA, THE FORMER KING.

THEN THE THRONE OF THE EMERALD CITY BELONGS TO THIS PASTORIA FROM WHOM THE WIZARD USURPED IT.

THAT'S TRUE. BUT PASTORIA IS NOW DEAD AND GONE, AND *SOMEONE* MUST RULE IN HIS PLACE.

PASTORIA HAD A DAUGHTER WHO IS THE RIGHTFUL HEIR TO THE THRONE OF THE EMERALD CITY. DID YOU KNOW THAT?

NO, BUT IF THE GIRL STILL LIVES I WON'T STAND IN HER WAY. IT WILL SATISFY ME TO HAVE JINJUR TURNED OUT, AS TO REGAIN THE THRONE MYSELF.

IN FACT, IT ISN'T MUCH FUN TO BE KING, ESPECIALLY IF ONE HAS GOOD BRAINS. I'VE KNOWN FOR SOME TIME THAT I'M FITTED TO OCCUPY A FAR MORE EXALTED POSITION.

BUT WHERE IS THE GIRL WHO OWNS THE THRONE, AND WHAT'S HER NAME?

HER NAME IS OZMA.

BUT WHERE SHE IS I'VE TRIED IN VAIN TO DISCOVER.

THE WIZARD OF OZ, WHEN HE STOLE THE THRONE FROM OZMA'S FATHER, HID THE GIRL IN SOME SECRET PLACE.

BY MEANS OF A MAGICAL TRICK WITH WHICH I'M NOT FAMILIAR HE ALSO MANAGED TO PREVENT HER BEING DISCOVERED --

-- EVEN BY SO EXPERIENCED A SORCERESS AS MYSELF.

THAT IS STRANGE. I'VE BEEN INFORMED THAT THE WONDERFUL WIZARD OF OZ WAS NOTHING MORE THAN A HUM-BUG!

NONSENSE! DIDN'T HE GIVE ME A WONDERFUL SET OF BRAINS?

THERE'S NO HUMBUG ABOUT MY HEART!

PERHAPS I WAS MISINFORMED -- I NEVER KNEW THE WIZARD PERSONALLY.

WELL, WE DID, AND HE WAS A VERY GREAT WIZARD, I ASSURE YOU.

IT'S TRUE HE WAS GUILTY OF SOME SLIGHT IMPOSTURES, BUT UNLESS HE WAS A GREAT WIZARD, HOW -- LET ME ASK -- COULD HE HAVE HIDDEN THIS GIRL OZMA SO SECURELY THAT NO ONE CAN FIND HER?

I -- I GIVE UP!

THAT'S THE MOST SENSIBLE SPEECH YOU'VE MADE.

I MUST MAKE ANOTHER EFFORT TO DISCOVER WHERE THIS GIRL IS HIDDEN. IN THE MEANTIME, AMUSE YOURSELVES IN MY PALACE. I'LL GRANT ANOTHER AUDIENCE TOMORROW.

IN GLINDA'S LIBRARY WAS A BOOK IN WHICH WAS INSCRIBED EVERY ACTION OF THE WIZARD IN THE LAND OF OZ -- AT LEAST, EVERY ACTION OBSERVED BY GLINDA'S SPIES.

THAT NIGHT SHE READ CAREFULLY.

THE FOLLOWING MORNING.

I'VE SEARCHED THROUGH THE RECORDS OF THE WIZARD'S ACTIONS, AND I CAN FIND BUT THREE THAT APPEAR TO HAVE BEEN SUSPICIOUS.

HE ATE BEANS WITH A KNIFE...

...MADE THREE SECRET VISITS TO OLD MOMBI...

...AND LIMPED SLIGHTLY ON HIS LEFT FOOT.

AH! THAT LAST IS CERTAINLY SUSPICIOUS!

NOT NECESSARILY— HE MAY HAVE HA CORNS. IT SEEM TO ME HIS EATIN BEANS WITH A KNIFE IS MORE SUSPICIOUS.

PERHAPS IT'S A POLITE CUSTOM IN OMAHA, FROM WHICH GREAT COUNTRY THE WIZARD ORIGINALLY CAME.

IT MAY BE.

THE WIZARD TAUGHT THE OLD WOMAN MANY OF HIS MAGIC TRICKS. THIS HE WOULDN'T HAVE DONE HAD SHE NOT ASSISTED HIM IN SOME WAY.

SO WE MAY SUSPECT WITH GOOD REASON THAT MOMB AIDED HIM TO HIDE THE GIRL OZMA, HEIR TO THE THRONE AND A CONSTANT DANGER TO THE USURPER.

BUT WHY DID HE MAKE THREE SECRET VISITS TO OLD MOMBI?

AH! WHY, INDEED!

FOR, IF THE PEOPLE KNEW THAT OZMA LIVED, THEY WOULD QUICKLY MAKE HER THEIR QUEEN.

I'VE NO DOUBT MOMBI WAS MIXED UP IN THIS WICKED BUSINESS. BUT HOW DOES THAT KNOWLEDGE HELP US?

WE MUST FIND MOMBI AND FORCE HER TO TELL WHERE THE GIRL IS HIDDEN.

MOMBI'S WITH QUEEN JINJUR IN THE EMERALD CITY.

SHE THREW OBSTACLES IN OUR PATHWAY AND MADE JINJUR THREATEN TO DESTROY MY FRIENDS AND GIVE ME BACK INTO THE OLD WITCH'S POWER.

THEN I'LL MARCH WITH MY ARMY TO THE EMERALD CITY AND TAKE MOMBI PRISONER. AFTER THAT WE CAN, PERHAPS, FORCE HER TO TELL THE TRUTH ABOUT OZMA.

SHE'S A TERRIBLE OLD WOMAN! AND OBSTINATE, TOO.

I'M QUITE OBSTINATE MYSELF, SO I DON'T FEAR MOMBI IN THE LEAST.

WE WILL MARCH AT DAYBREAK TOMORROW.

THE ARMY OF GLINDA THE GOOD ASSEMBLED AT DAYBREAK BEFORE THE PALACE GATES AND MARCHED SWIFTLY AWAY.

THE SORCERESS RODE IN A BEAUTIFUL PALANQUIN...

...WHILE THE GUMP FLEW DIRECTLY OVER THE PALANQUIN.

BE CAREFUL LEANING OVER THE SIDE, SCARECROW-- YOU MIGHT FALL!

IT WOULDN'T MATTER -- HE CAN'T GET BROKE SO LONG AS HE'S STUFFED WITH MONEY.

DIDN'T I ASK YOU --

YOU DID! I BEG YOUR PARDON. I WILL REALLY TRY TO RESTRAIN MYSELF.

YOU'D BETTER.

NIGHT HAD FALLEN BEFORE THEY CAME TO THE WALLS OF THE EMERALD CITY.

NEXT MORNING.

WE ARE LOST!

HOW CAN OUR KNITTING-NEEDLES AVAIL AGAINST LONG SPEARS AND TERRIBLE SWORDS?

THE BEST THING WE CAN DO IS TO SURRENDER, BEFORE WE GET HURT.

NOT SO! THE ENEMY IS STILL OUTSIDE THE WALLS.

WE MUST TRY TO GAIN TIME BY ENGAGING THEM IN PARLEY.

GO WITH A FLAG OF TRUCE TO GLINDA AND ASK HER WHY SHE HAS DARED TO INVADE MY DOMINIONS, AND WHAT ARE HER DEMANDS.

So THE GIRL PASSED THROUGH THE GATES.

TELL YOUR QUEEN THAT SHE MUST DELIVER UP TO ME OLD MOMBI. IF THIS IS DONE I WILL NOT MOLEST HER FURTHER.

JINJUR SENT FOR MOMBI AND TOLD HER WHAT GLINDA HAD SAID.

IN MY MAGIC MIRROR I SEE TROUBLE FOR ALL OF US AHEAD. BUT WE MAY EVEN YET ESCAPE BY DECEIVING THIS SORCERESS, CLEVER AS SHE THINKS HERSELF.

DON'T YOU THINK IT WILL BE SAFER FOR ME TO DELIVER YOU INTO HER HANDS?

IF YOU DO, IT WILL COST YOU THE THRONE OF THE EMERALD CITY!

BUT IF YOU'LL LET ME HAVE MY OWN WAY, I CAN SAVE US BOTH VERY EASILY.

THEN DO AS YOU PLEASE. FOR IT IS *SO* ARISTOCRATIC TO BE A QUEEN -- I DON'T WISH TO RETURN HOME TO MAKE BEDS AND WASH DISHES FOR MY MOTHER.

*S*O MOMBI CALLED JELLIA JAMB AND PERFORMED A CERTAIN MAGICAL RITE.

HEE HEE HEE HEE HEE HEE!

MY, AIN'T I JUST TOO KILLING IN THIS DRESS?

HEE HEE *HEE* HEE HEE HEE!

OH!

CONFESS THIS FRAUD TO GLINDA AND YOU SHALL MEET *DEATH!*

LET YOUR SOLDIERS DELIVER THIS GIRL TO GLINDA. SHE'LL THINK SHE HAS THE REAL MOMBI AND WILL RETURN TO HER OWN COUNTRY.

HERE IS THE PERSON YOU DEMANDED. OUR QUEEN NOW BEGS YOU'LL GO AWAY, AS YOU PROMISED.

THAT I'LL DO...IF THIS IS THE PERSON SHE SEEMS TO BE.

NOW MOMBI, THE DAY OF RECKONING IS AT HAND. TELL ME ALL YOU KNOW ABOUT THE LOST GIRL OZMA.

BUT JELLIA KNEW NOTHING AT ALL OF THE AFFAIR.

HERE'S SOME FOOLISH TRICKERY! THIS IS NOT MOMBI AT ALL, BUT SOME OTHER PERSON WHO HAS BEEN MADE TO RESEMBLE HER.

WHY, IT'S JELLIA JAMB!

OUR INTERPRETER!

AT THE SAME TIME IN JINJUR'S PALACE...

IT'S A TRICK MOMBI PLAYED -- SHE THREATENED ME WITH DEATH. I BEG YOUR PROTECTION, GREAT SORCERESS.

READILY GRANTED.

BUT JINJUR MUST DELIVER UP THE REAL MOMBI OR SUFFER TERRIBLE CONSEQUENCES.

GLINDA SENT WORD TO JINJUR.

TELL YOUR MISTRESS THAT I CANNOT FIND MOMBI ANYWHERE. GLINDA IS WELCOME TO ENTER THE CITY AND SEARCH FOR THE OLD WOMAN.

SHE MAY ALSO BRING HER FRIENDS WITH HER.

BUT IF SHE DOESN'T FIND MOMBI BY SUNDOWN, THE SORCERESS MUST PROMISE TO GO AWAY AND BOTHER US NO MORE.

GLINDA AGREED TO THESE TERMS, WELL KNOWING THAT MOMBI WAS SOMEWHERE WITHIN THE CITY WALLS.

MEANWHILE, IN THE GARDEN OF THE PALACE...

I'VE NO INTENTION OF BEING FOUND BY GLINDA.

AS TRANSFORMATIONS WERE EASY TO HER, THE WITCH TRANSFORMED HERSELF.

IT WAS A TRICK GLINDA DID NOT SUSPECT, SO SEVERAL HOURS WERE SPENT IN A VAIN SEARCH.

AS SUNDOWN APPROACHED...

I'VE BEEN DEFEATED BY SUPERIOR CUNNING. I GIVE THE COMMAND TO MARCH OUT OF THE CITY AND BACK TO OUR TENTS.

THE SCARECROW AND HIS COMRADES TURNED WITH DISAPPOINTMENT TO OBEY.

AH! WHAT A BIG RED ROSE!

UHHHH...

MOMBI WAS CARRIED OUT OF THE CITY WITHOUT ANYONE SUSPECTING THAT THEY'D SUCCEEDED IN THEIR QUEST.

I'VE BEEN CAPTURED BY THE ENEMY...

...BUT I SEEM TO BE EXACTLY AS SAFE HERE AS GROWING UPON THE BUSH.

AND NOW THAT I'M OUTSIDE THE CITY, MY CHANCES OF ESCAPING FROM GLINDA ARE MUCH IMPROVED.

BUT THERE'S NO HURRY.

I'LL WAIT AND ENJOY THE HUMILIATION OF THE SORCERESS WHEN SHE FINDS I'VE OUTWITTED HER.

IN THE MORNING GLINDA SUMMONED OUR FRIENDS TO HER TENT.

FOR SOME REASON WE'VE FAILED TO FIND THIS CUNNING OLD MOMBI. I FEAR OUR EXPEDITION WILL PROVE A FAILURE.

FOR THAT I'M SORRY, BECAUSE WITHOUT OUR ASSISTANCE LITTLE OZMA WILL NEVER BE RESTORED TO HER RIGHTFUL POSITION AS QUEEN OF THE EMERALD CITY.

DON'T GIVE UP SO EASILY.

I BELIEVE IT WOULD BE WISE FOR US TO CONQUER THE EMERALD CITY FOR PRINCESS OZMA AND FIND THE GIRL AFTERWARD.

WHILE THE GIRL REMAINS HIDDEN, I'LL GLADLY RULE IN HER PLACE. I UNDERSTAND THE BUSINESS MUCH BETTER THAN JINJUR.

BUT I'VE PROMISED NOT TO MOLEST JINJUR. I CANNOT UNDERSTAND HOW I'VE BEEN DEFEATED BY AN OLD WITCH WHO KNOWS FAR LESS OF MAGIC THAN I DO.

SUPPOSE YOU ALL RETURN WITH ME TO MY CASTLE, WHERE THERE'S ROOM ENOUGH AND TO SPARE.

AND IF ANY OF YOU WISH TO BE NICKEL-PLATED, MY VALET WILL DO IT FREE OF EXPENSE.

*W*HILE THE WOODMAN WAS SPEAKING, GLINDA NOTED THE ROSE AND SAW THE FLOWER TREMBLE SLIGHTLY.

THAT ROSE... IS NOTHING ELSE THAN A TRANSFORMATION OF OLD MOMBI!

I'M DISCOVERED!

MOMBI IMMEDIATELY TOOK THE FORM OF A SHADOW.

REMAIN PERFECTLY QUIET, ALL OF YOU!

THE OLD WITCH IS EVEN NOW WITH US IN THE TENT!

MOMBI QUICKLY TRANSFORMED HERSELF TO A BLACK ANT, SEEKING A CRACK OR CREVICE TO HIDE.

I HOPE TO CAPTURE HER!

THE WITCH, FRANTIC WITH FEAR, MADE HER LAST TRANSFORMATION -- THE FORM OF A GRIFFIN.

AWK!

RRPPRIP!

NOW, SAW-HORSE, YOU SHALL PROVE THAT YOU HAVE A RIGHT TO BE ALIVE! *RUN!*

RUN! RUN!

COME! LET'S FOLLOW!

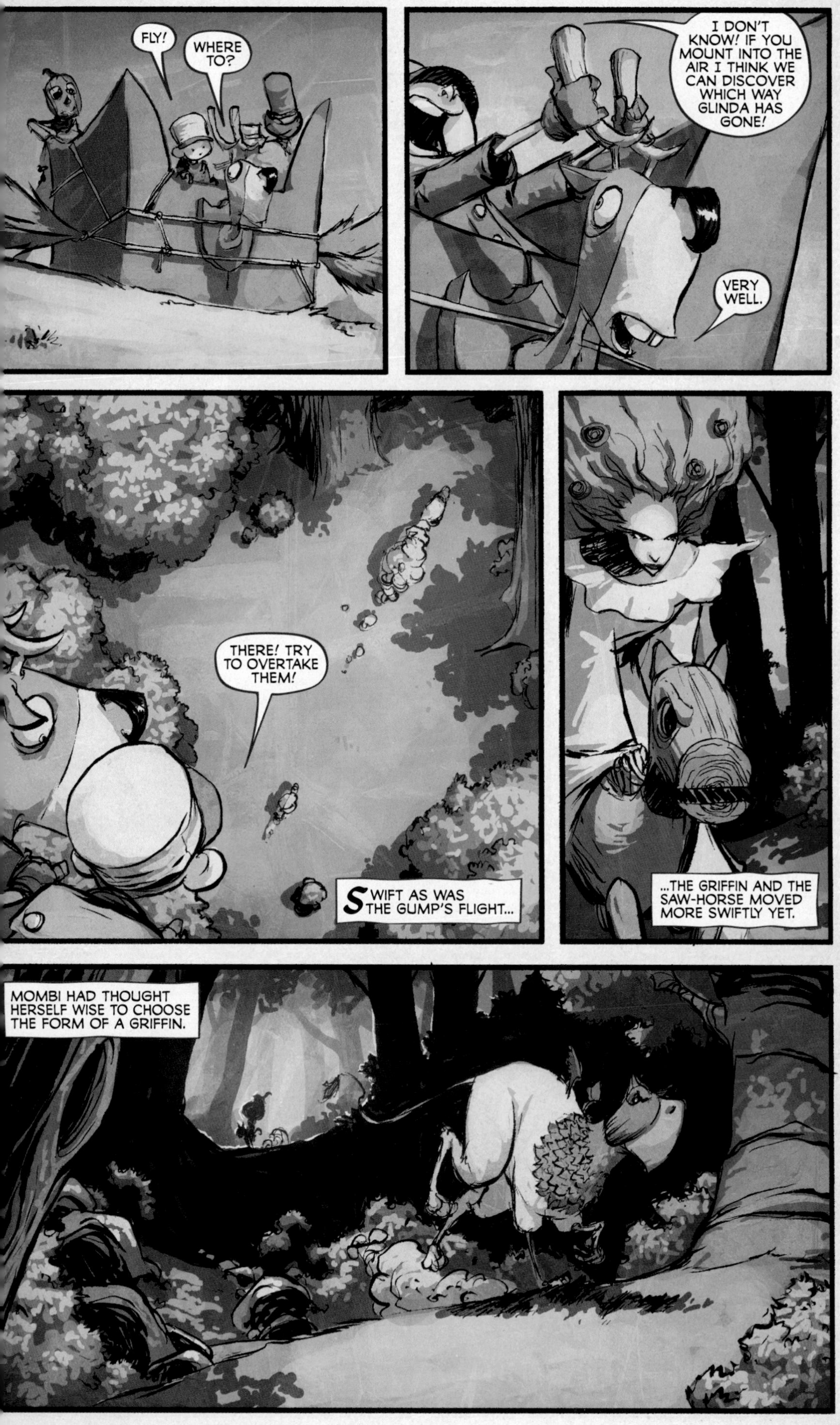
FLY!
WHERE TO?
I DON'T KNOW! IF YOU MOUNT INTO THE AIR I THINK WE CAN DISCOVER WHICH WAY GLINDA HAS GONE!
VERY WELL.
THERE! TRY TO OVERTAKE THEM!
SWIFT AS WAS THE GUMP'S FLIGHT...
...THE GRIFFIN AND THE SAW-HORSE MOVED MORE SWIFTLY YET.
MOMBI HAD THOUGHT HERSELF WISE TO CHOOSE THE FORM OF A GRIFFIN.

ITS LEGS WERE EXCEEDINGLY FLEET AND ITS STRENGTH MORE ENDURING THAN THAT OF OTHER ANIMALS.

BUT SHE HADN'T RECKONED ON THE UNTIRING WOODEN LIMBS OF THE SAW-HORSE.

Huh--

Huh--

Huh--

Huh--

Huh--

Huff--

HUFF--

HUFF--

HUUUuuuhhh...

--hurk!

YOU'RE MY PRISONER—IT'S USELESS TO STRUGGLE.

HUH...

HUH...

WHAT HAVE I DONE TO YOU, TO BE SO PERSECUTED?

YOU'VE DONE NOTHING TO ME.

BUT I SUSPECT YOU'VE BEEN GUILTY OF SEVERAL WICKED ACTIONS.

IF I FIND IT'S TRUE THAT YOU'VE SO ABUSED YOUR KNOWLEDGE OF MAGIC, I INTEND TO PUNISH YOU SEVERELY.

I DEFY YOU! YOU DARE NOT HARM ME!

*I*T WAS DECIDED THEY SHOULD ALL RETURN TO CAMP IN THE GUMP.

HOORAY!

NOW, I WANT YOU TO TELL US WHY THE WONDERFUL WIZARD OF OZ PAID YOU THREE VISITS AND WHAT BECAME OF THE CHILD OZMA.

ANSWER ME!

PERHAPS SHE DOESN'T KNOW.

KEEP QUIET! YOU MIGHT SPOIL EVERYTHING!

VERY WELL, DEAR FATHER.

HOW GLAD I AM TO BE A WOGGLE-BUG. NO ONE CAN EXPECT WISDOM FROM A PUMPKIN.

WELL, WHAT SHALL WE DO TO MAKE MOMBI SPEAK?

I'VE HEARD THAT ANYONE CAN BE CONQUERED WITH KIND-NESS...

YOU'LL GAIN NOTHING BY DEFYING US.

UNLESS YOU TELL ME THE TRUTH ABOUT THE GIRL OZMA, I'LL CERTAINLY PUT YOU TO DEATH.

...NO MATTER HOW UGLY THEY MAY BE.

DON'T DO THAT! IT WOULD BE AWFUL TO KILL ANYONE -- EVEN OLD MOMBI!

IT'S MERELY A THREAT. I SHALL NOT PUT MOMBI TO DEATH, BECAUSE SHE WILL PREFER TO TELL THE TRUTH.

OH, I SEE!

SUPPOSE I TELL YOU ALL YOU WISH TO KNOW. WHAT WILL YOU DO WITH ME THEN?

I SHALL MERELY ASK YOU TO DRINK A POWERFUL DRAUGHT WHICH WILL CAUSE YOU TO FORGET ALL THE MAGIC YOU'VE EVER LEARNED.

THEN I'D BECOME A HELPLESS OLD WOMAN!

BUT YOU'D BE ALIVE.

KEEP SILENT!

I'LL TRY -- BUT IT'S A GOOD THING TO BE ALIVE.

ESPECIALLY IF ONE HAPPENS TO BE THOROUGHLY EDUCATED.

YOU MAY MAKE YOUR CHOICE... ...BETWEEN DEATH IF YOU REMAIN SILENT -- AND LOSS OF YOUR MAGICAL POWERS IF YOU TELL THE TRUTH...

...BUT I THINK YOU' PREFER TO LIVE.

I'LL ANSWER YOUR QUESTIONS.

THAT'S WHAT I EXPECTED. YOU'VE CHOSEN WISELY, I ASSURE YOU.

NOW I'LL ASK MY FIRST QUESTION: WHY DID THE WIZARD PAY YOU THREE VISITS?

BECAUSE I WOULDN'T COME TO HIM.

THAT IS NO ANSWER TELL ME THE TRUTH.

WE-E-E-E-LLLLLL...

...HE VISITED ME TO LEARN THE WAY I MAKE TEA-BISCUITS.

WHAT IS THE COLOR OF MY PEARL?

WHY--IT'S BLACK!

YOU'VE TOLD ME A FALSEHOOD! ONLY WHEN THE TRUTH IS SPOKEN WILL MY MAGIC PEARL REMAIN PURE WHITE!

THE WIZARD BROUGHT ME THE GIRL OZMA, WHO WAS THEN NO MORE THAN A BABY, AND BEGGED ME TO CONCEAL THE CHILD.

WHAT DID HE GIVE YOU FOR SERVING HIM?

HE TAUGHT ME ALL THE MAGICAL TRICKS HE KNEW. SOME WERE GOOD, SOME ONLY FRAUDS. BUT I'VE REMAINED FAITHFUL TO MY PROMISE.

WHAT DID YOU DO WITH THE GIRL?

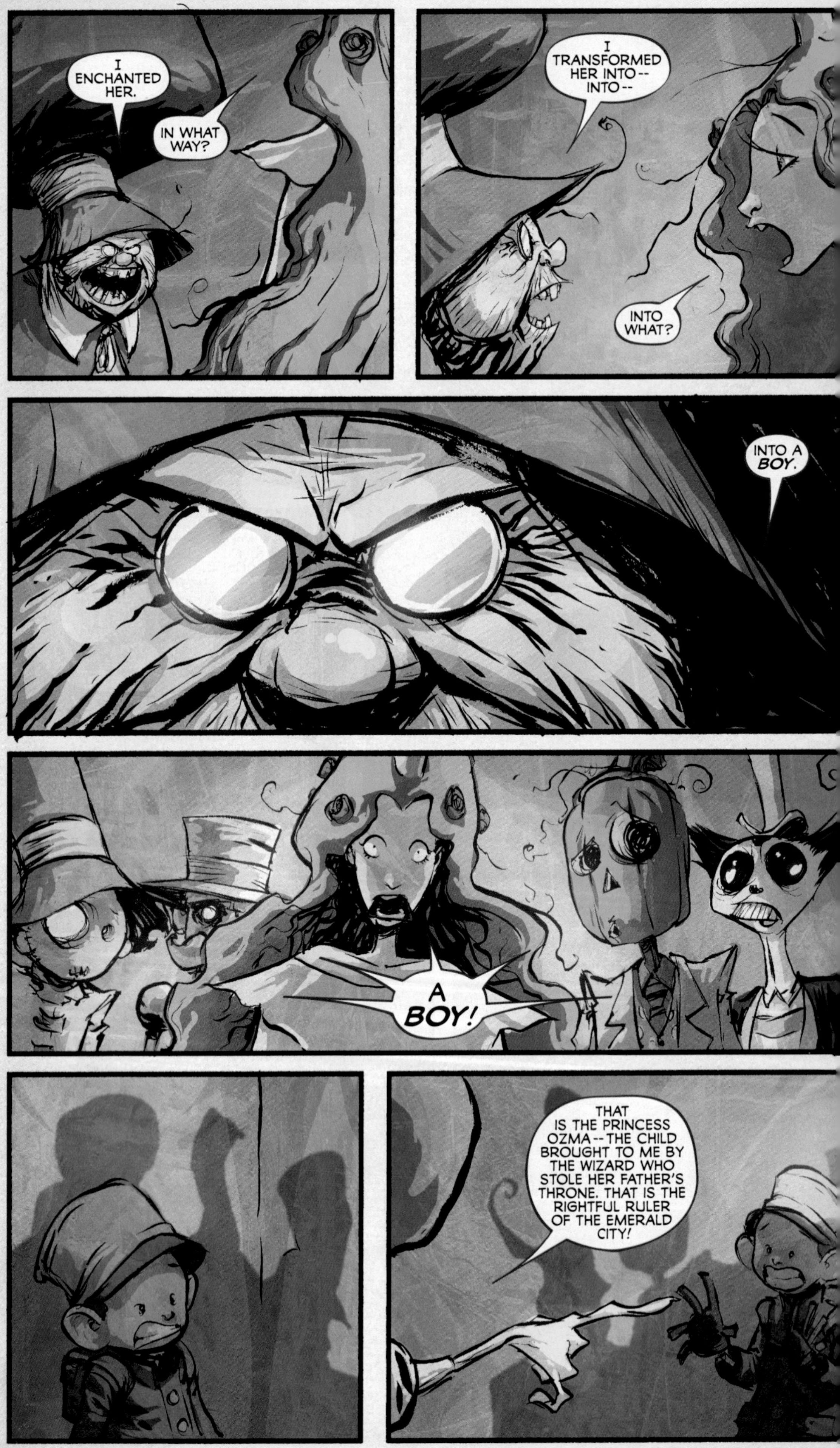
I ENCHANTED HER.
IN WHAT WAY?
I TRANSFORMED HER INTO-- INTO--
INTO WHAT?
INTO A *BOY*.
A *BOY*!
THAT IS THE PRINCESS OZMA--THE CHILD BROUGHT TO ME BY THE WIZARD WHO STOLE HER FATHER'S THRONE. THAT IS THE RIGHTFUL RULER OF THE EMERALD CITY!

I--I'M NO PRINCESS OZMA--I'M NOT A GIRL!

YOU'RE NOT A GIRL JUST NOW BECAUSE MOMBI TRANSFORMED YOU. BUT YOU WERE BORN A GIRL, SO YOU MUST RESUME YOUR PROPER FORM TO BECOME QUEEN OF THE EMERALD CITY.

LET JINJUR BE THE QUEEN!

I WANT TO STAY A BOY--AND TRAVEL WITH THE SCARECROW AND THE TIN WOODMAN AND THE WOGGLE-BUG AND JACK--I DON'T WANT TO BE A GIRL!

IT DOESN'T HURT TO BE A GIRL, I'M TOLD. AND WE'LL REMAIN YOUR FAITHFUL FRIENDS. TO BE HONEST, I'VE ALWAYS CONSIDERED GIRLS NICER THAN BOYS.

JUST AS NICE, ANYWAY.

AND EQUALLY GOOD STUDENTS. I'D LIKE TO BE YOUR TUTOR WHEN YOU'RE TRANSFORMED INTO A GIRL AGAIN.

BUT IF YOU BECOME A GIRL, YOU CAN'T BE MY DEAR FATHER ANY MORE!

NO--AND I WON'T BE SORRY TO ESCAPE THE RELATIONSHIP!

I--I MIGHT TRY IT FOR AWHILE--JUST TO SEE HOW IT SEEMS, YOU KNOW.

BUT IF I DON'T LIKE BEING A GIRL YOU MUST PROMISE TO CHANGE ME INTO A BOY AGAIN.

REALLY THAT'S BEYOND MY MAGIC. I NEVER DEAL IN TRANSFORMATIONS, FOR THEY'RE NOT HONEST.

I MUST ASK MOMBI TO EFFECT YOUR RELEASE FROM HER CHARM. IT WILL BE THE LAST OPPORTUNITY SHE'LL HAVE TO PRACTICE MAGIC.

MOMBI DID NOT CARE WHAT BECAME OF TIP, BUT SHE FEARED GLINDA'S ANGER, SO SHE CONSENTED TO EFFECT THE TRANSFORMATION.

SIZZLE

THAT POTION WILL SEND HIM INTO A DEEP AND DREAMLESS SLEEP.

WOOSH!

YEOWA!

I HOPE NONE OF YOU WILL CARE LESS FOR ME THAN YOU DID BEFORE.

I'M JUST THE SAME TIP, YOU KNOW -- ONLY -- ONLY --

ONLY YOU'RE DIFFERENT!

AND EVERYONE THOUGHT THAT WAS THE WISEST SPEECH HE'D EVER MADE.

THE TIDINGS REACHED QUEEN JINJUR.

TO THINK THAT AFTER HAVING RULED AS QUEEN, I MUST GO BACK TO SCRUBBING FLOORS AND CHURNING BUTTER! IT'S TOO HORRIBLE TO THINK OF!

RESIST!

SCRATCH THEIR EYES OUT!

WE'RE BEING ROBBED!

I'LL NEVER CONSENT! CLOSE AND BAR EVERY GATEWAY OF THE EMERALD CITY!

THE NEXT DAY WITH A DECLARATION OF WAR GLINDA MARCHED UPON THE CITY.

BUT AT THE WALLS THE ADVANCE WAS BAFFLED.

WE MUST LAY SIEGE TO THE CITY AND STARVE IT INTO SUBMISSION. IT'S THE ONLY THING WE CAN DO.

NOT SO! WE STILL HAVE THE GUMP AND THE GUMP CAN STILL FLY.

YOU'RE RIGHT! YOU CERTAINLY HAVE REASON TO BE PROUD OF YOUR BRAINS.

OON...

HANDS OFF! HOW DARE YOU TREAT ME SO ROUGHLY!

THAT ACT REALLY ENDED THE WAR.

HERALDS PROCLAIMED THE CONQUEST OF JINJUR AND THE ACCESSION OF PRINCESS OZMA TO THE THRONE OF HER ROYAL ANCESTORS.

THE MEN OF THE EMERALD CITY CAST OFF THEIR APRONS.

THE WOMEN--TIRED OF EATING THEIR HUSBANDS' COOKING--PREPARED SO DELICIOUS A FEAST THAT HARMONY WAS RESTORED IN EVERY FAMILY.

OZMA'S FIRST ACT WAS TO OBLIGE THE RETURN OF EVERY GEM STOLEN FROM THE PUBLIC STREETS. THE ROYAL JEWELERS WORKED STEADILY FOR MORE THAN A MONTH TO REPLACE THEM.

THE ARMY OF REVOLT WAS DISBANDED AND THE GIRLS SENT HOME TO THEIR MOTHERS.

NEVER! I'LL GET A PENSION AND RETIRE.

ON PROMISE OF GOOD BEHAVIOR JINJUR WAS LIKEWISE RELEASED.

I'LL MARRY! THERE'S MORE THAN *ONE* WAY TO WIN BATTLES.

LINDA CAUSED MOMBI TO FORGET ALL HER WITCHCRAFT, AND OZMA GENEROUSLY PROMISED TO PROVIDE FOR MOMBI IN HER OLD AGE.

OLD MOMBI HAS HAD HER DAY-- IT WAS GOOD FUN WHILE IT LASTED.

PEACE WAS RESTORED TO THE EMERALD CITY, AND GLINDA'S ARMY MARCHED BACK HOME....

OZMA WAS GRATEFUL TO THE GUMP AND OFFERED IT ANY REWARD IT MIGHT NAME.

I DIDN'T WISH TO BE BROUGHT TO LIFE AND I'M GREATLY ASHAMED OF MY CONGLOMERATE PERSONALITY.

THERE-FORE I BEG TO BE DISPERSED PLEASE TAKE ME TO PIECES.

THE SOFAS WERE UNTIED AND PLACED IN RECEPTION PARLORS.

♪♪♪

THE BROOM TAIL RESUMED ITS ACCUSTOMED DUTIES.

THE SCARECROW REPLACED ALL THE CLOTHESLINES AND ROPES. AND THE HEAD WAS AGAIN HUNG OVER THE MANTELPIECE IN THE HALL...

...WHERE IT STARTLED VISITORS BY ASKING ABRUPT QUESTIONS.

YOU DON'T THINK I DO THIS ON PURPOSE, DO YOU?

JACK PUMPKINHEAD DID NOT SPOIL AS SOON AS HE FEARED.

THE WOGGLE-BUG -- APPOINTED TO THE POST OF PUBLIC EDUCATOR -- TRIED TO TEACH HIM SEVERAL ARTS AND SCIENCES.

BUT JACK WAS SO POOR A STUDENT THAT ANY ATTEMPT TO EDUCATE HIM WAS SOON ABANDONED.

OZMA MADE THE LOVELIEST QUEEN THE EMERALD CITY HAD EVER KNOWN.

ALTHOUGH SHE WAS YOUNG AND INEXPERIENCED, SHE PROVED HER ROYAL BLOOD BY RULING WITH WISDOM AND JUSTICE.

SHE HAD THE SAW-HORSE'S WOODEN LEGS SHOD WITH GOLD TO KEEP THEM FROM WEARING OUT.

TINK TINKLE TINK

THIS EVIDENCE OF HER MAGICAL POWERS FILLED THE QUEEN'S SUBJECTS WITH AWE.

THE WONDERFUL WIZARD WAS NEVER SO WONDERFUL AS QUEEN OZMA.

HE CLAIMED TO DO THINGS HE COULDN'T, BUT OUR NEW QUEEN DOES THINGS NO ONE WOULD EXPECT.

THE TIN WOODMAN ANNOUNCED HIS INTENTION TO RETURN TO HIS KINGDOM OF THE WINKIES.

WHEN I GET HOME I SHALL HAVE A NEW COAT OF NICKELPLATE, FOR I'VE BECOME SCRATCHED LATELY.

AND THEN I'LL BE GLAD TO HAVE YOU PAY ME A VISIT.

THANK YOU.

AND I SHALL NEVER BE PARTED FROM MY FRIEND THE TIN WOOD-MAN.

I'VE MADE THE SCARECROW MY ROYAL TREASURER, FOR IT'S A GOOD THING TO HAVE A TREASURER MADE OF MONEY. WHAT DO YOU THINK?

I THINK THAT YOUR FRIEND MUST BE THE RICHEST MAN IN ALL THE WORLD.

BUT NOT ON ACCOUNT OF MY MONEY. I CONSIDER BRAINS SUPERIOR TO MONEY.

IF ONE HAS MONEY WITHOUT BRAINS, HE CAN'T USE IT TO ADVANTAGE. BUT BRAINS WITHOUT MONEY ENABLE ONE TO LIVE COMFORTABLY TO THE END OF HIS DAYS.

AT THE SAME TIME, YOU MUST ACKNOWLEDGE THAT A GOOD HEART IS A THING BRAINS CAN'T CREATE AND MONEY CAN'T BUY.

PERHAPS IT'S I WHO AM THE RICHEST MAN IN ALL THE WORLD.

YOU ARE BOTH RICH, MY FRIENDS, AND YOUR RICHES ARE THE ONLY RICHES WORTH HAVING --

-- THE RICHES OF CONTENT!

THE END

THE STORY CONTINUES IN...

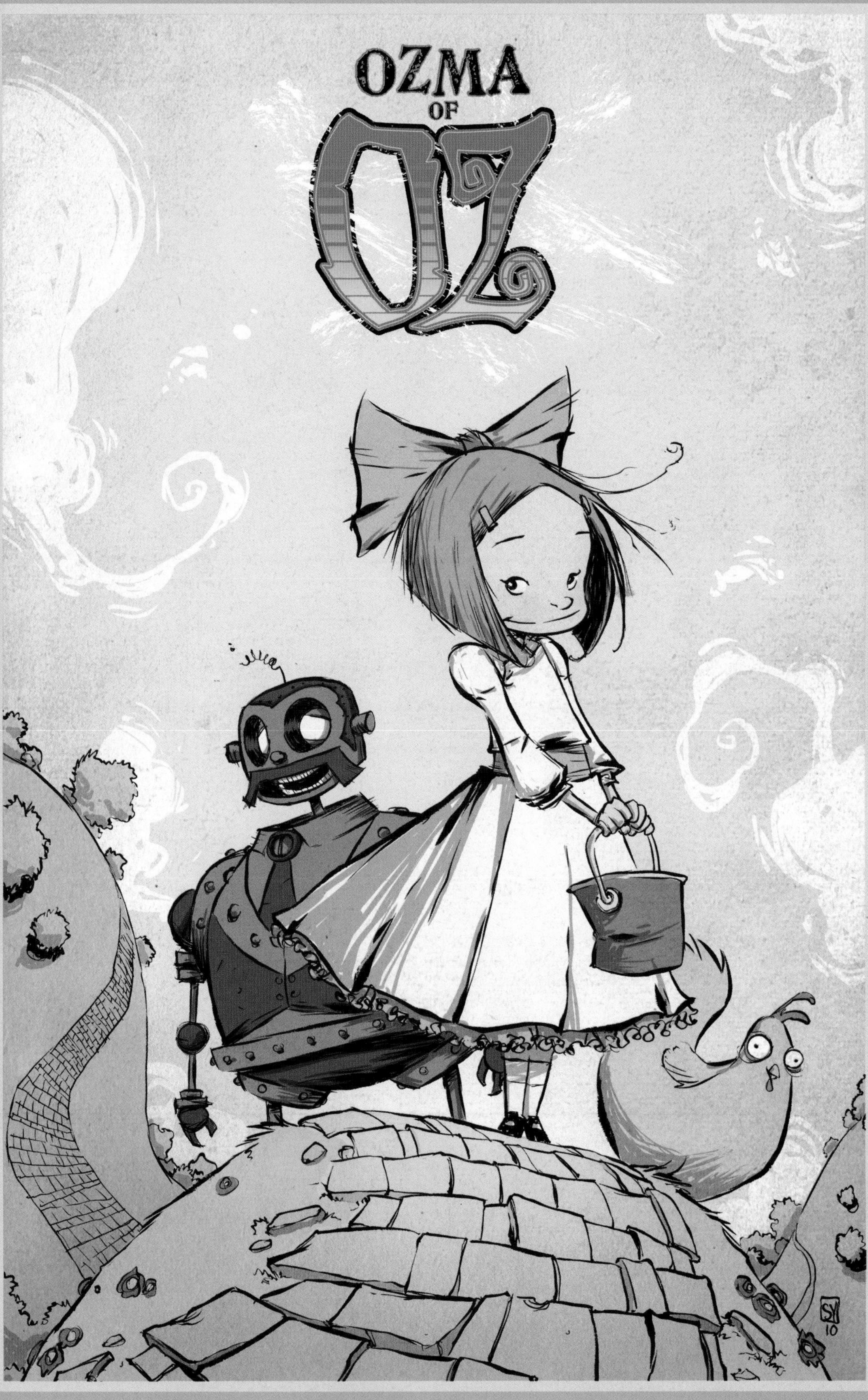
OZMA
OF
OZ
SY
10

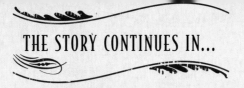

ONE

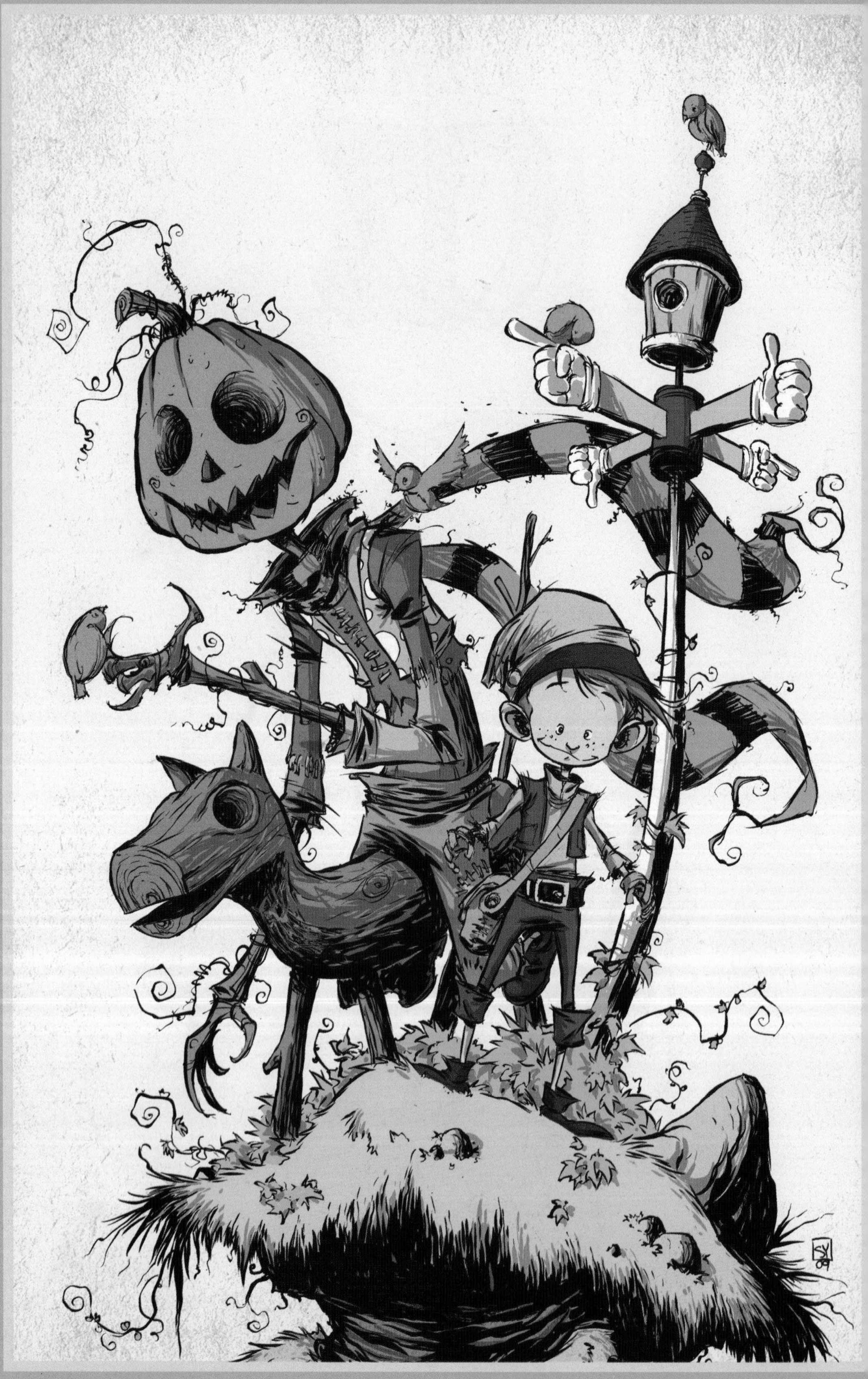

ONE

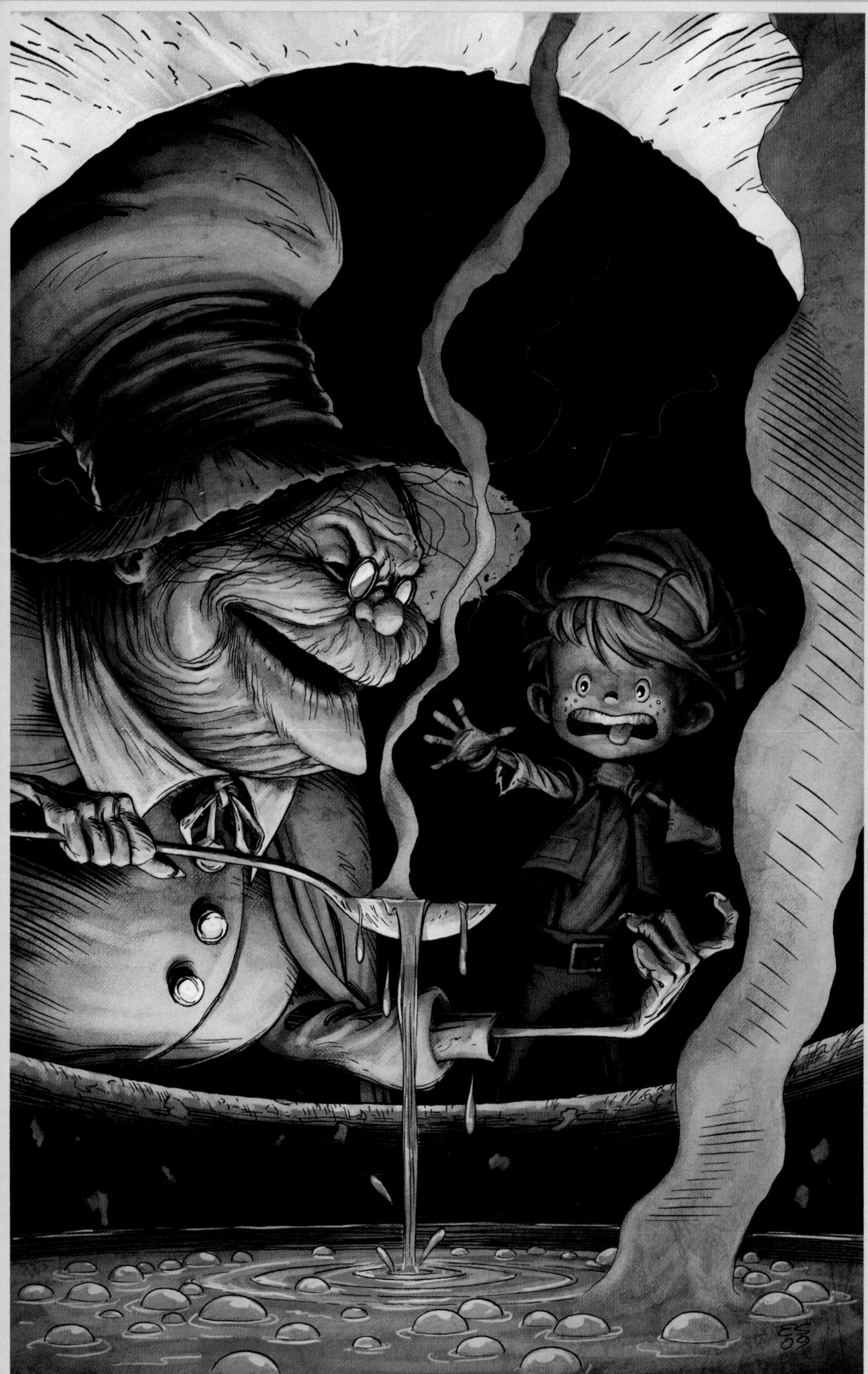

EC
09

Variant Cover by Eric Shanower

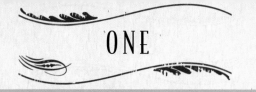

VARIANT COVER BY ED McGUINNESS

ONE

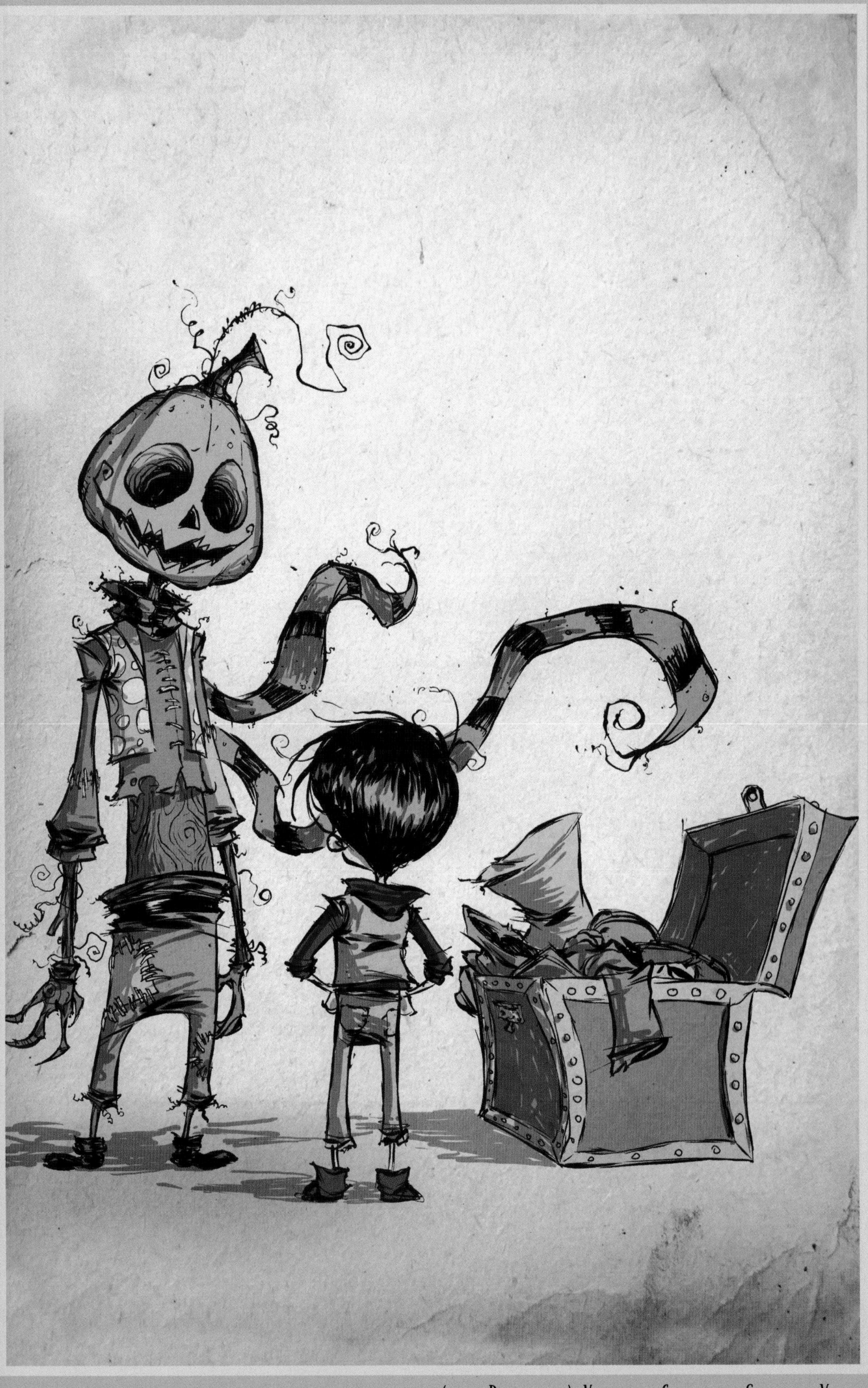

(2nd Printing) Variant Cover by Skottie Young

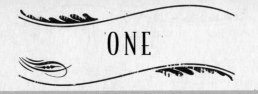

TWO

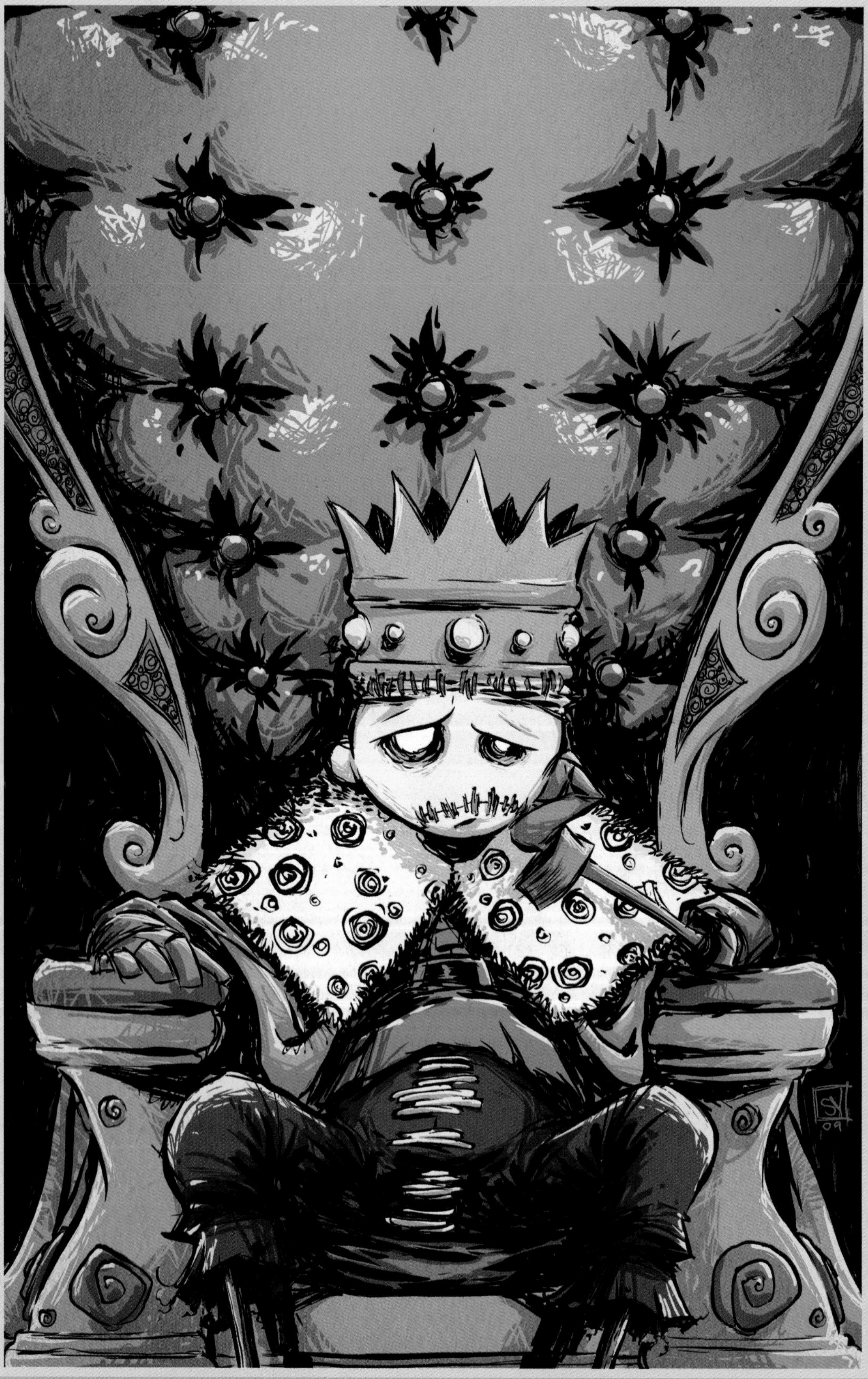

THREE

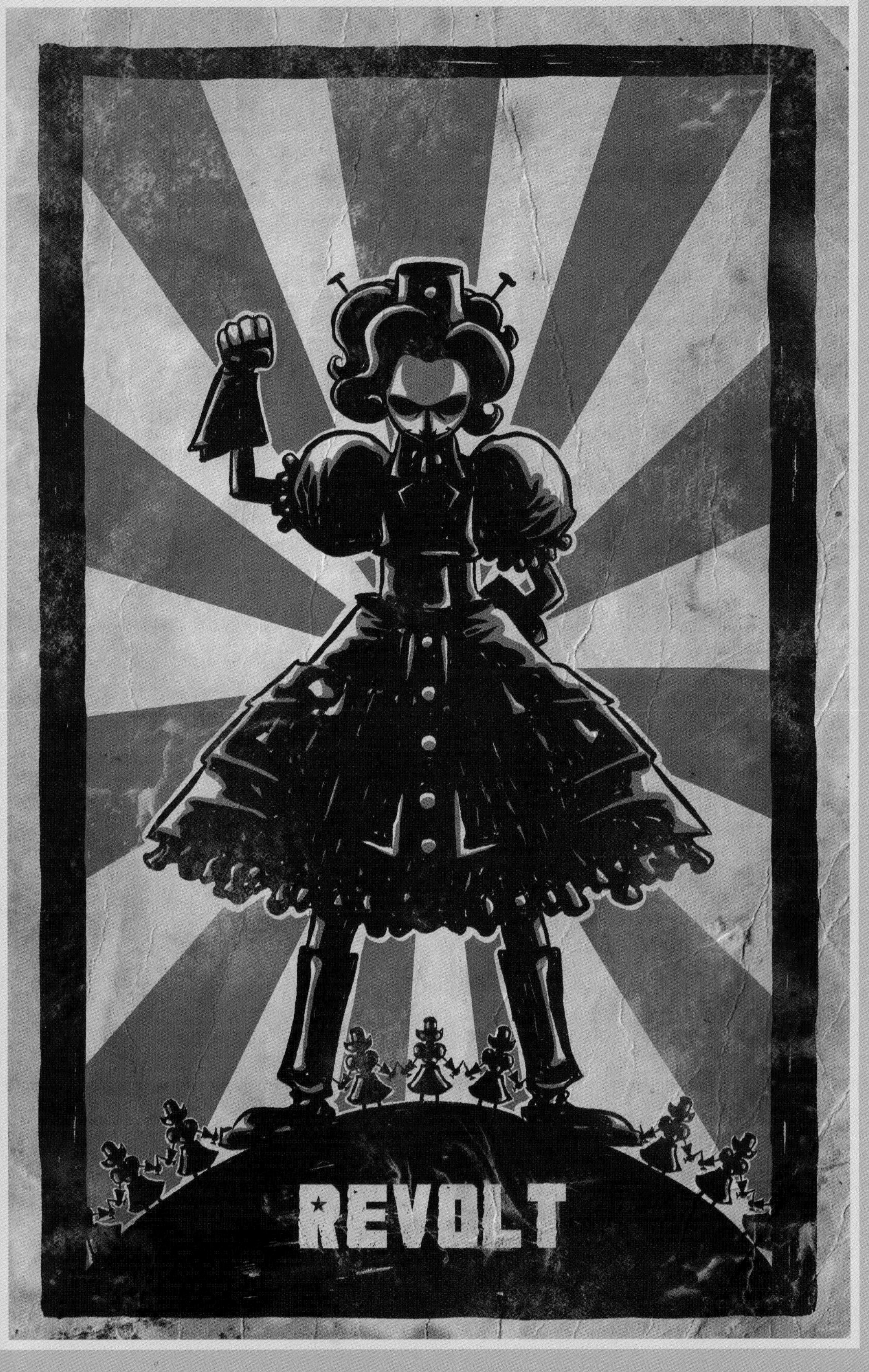
REVOLT

FOUR

chirpity chirp

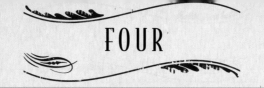

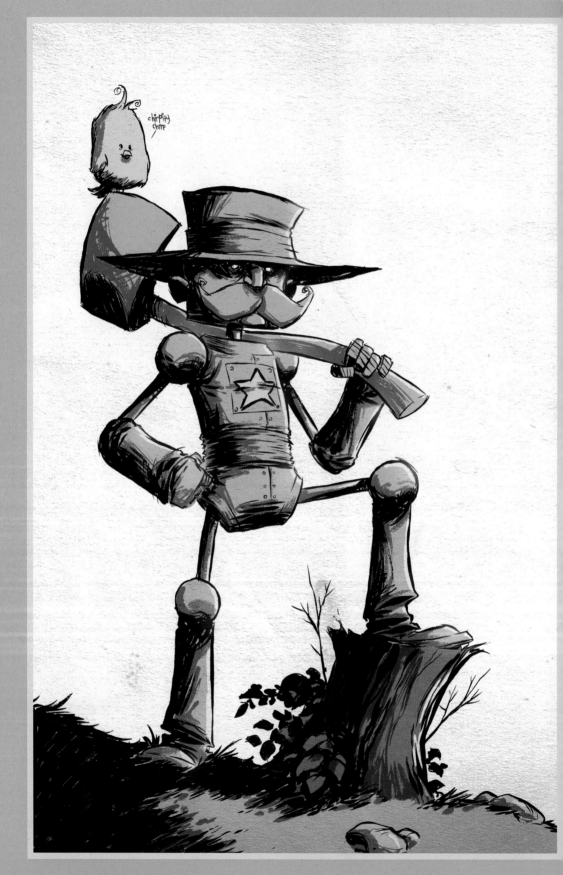

FIVE

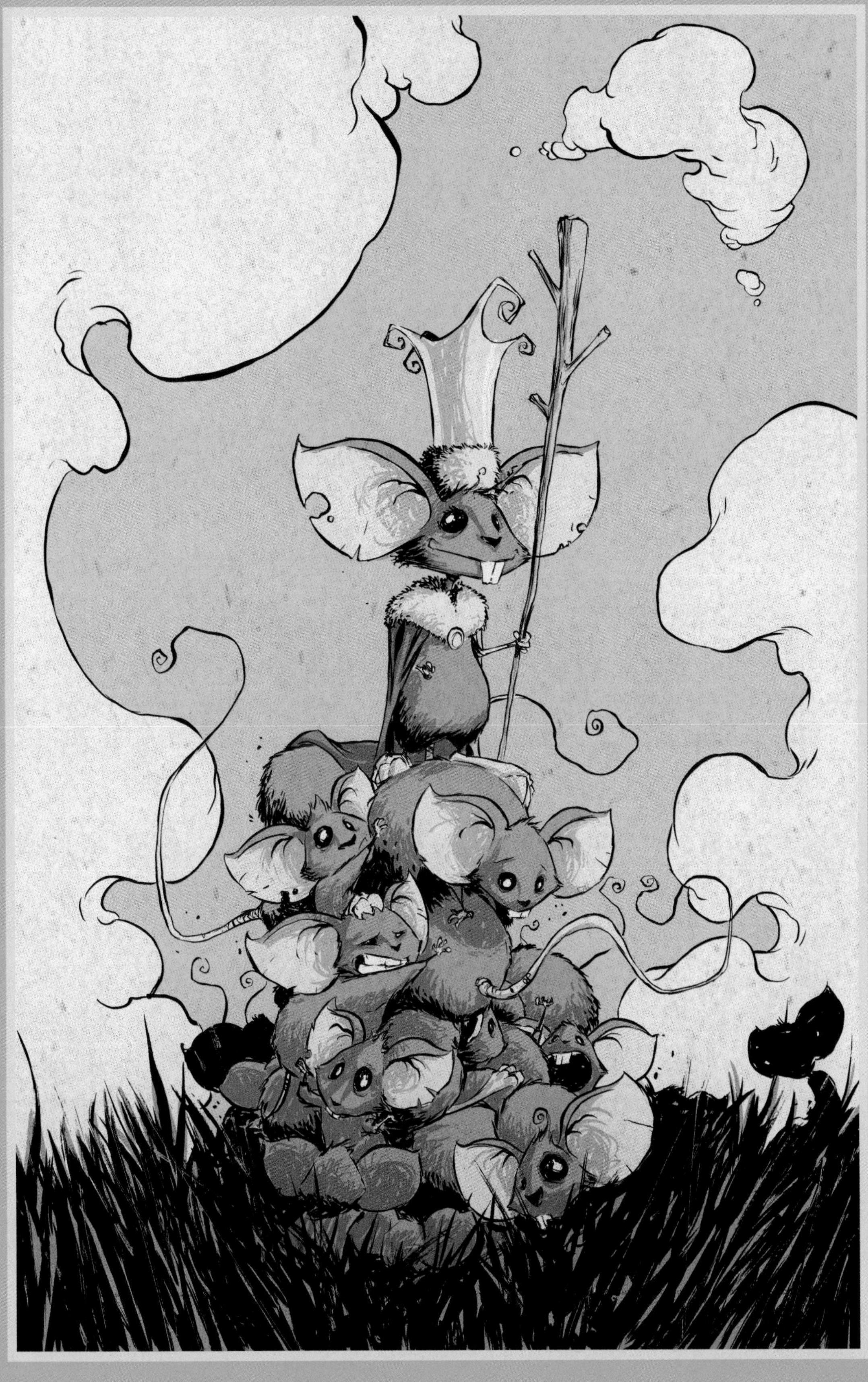

SIX

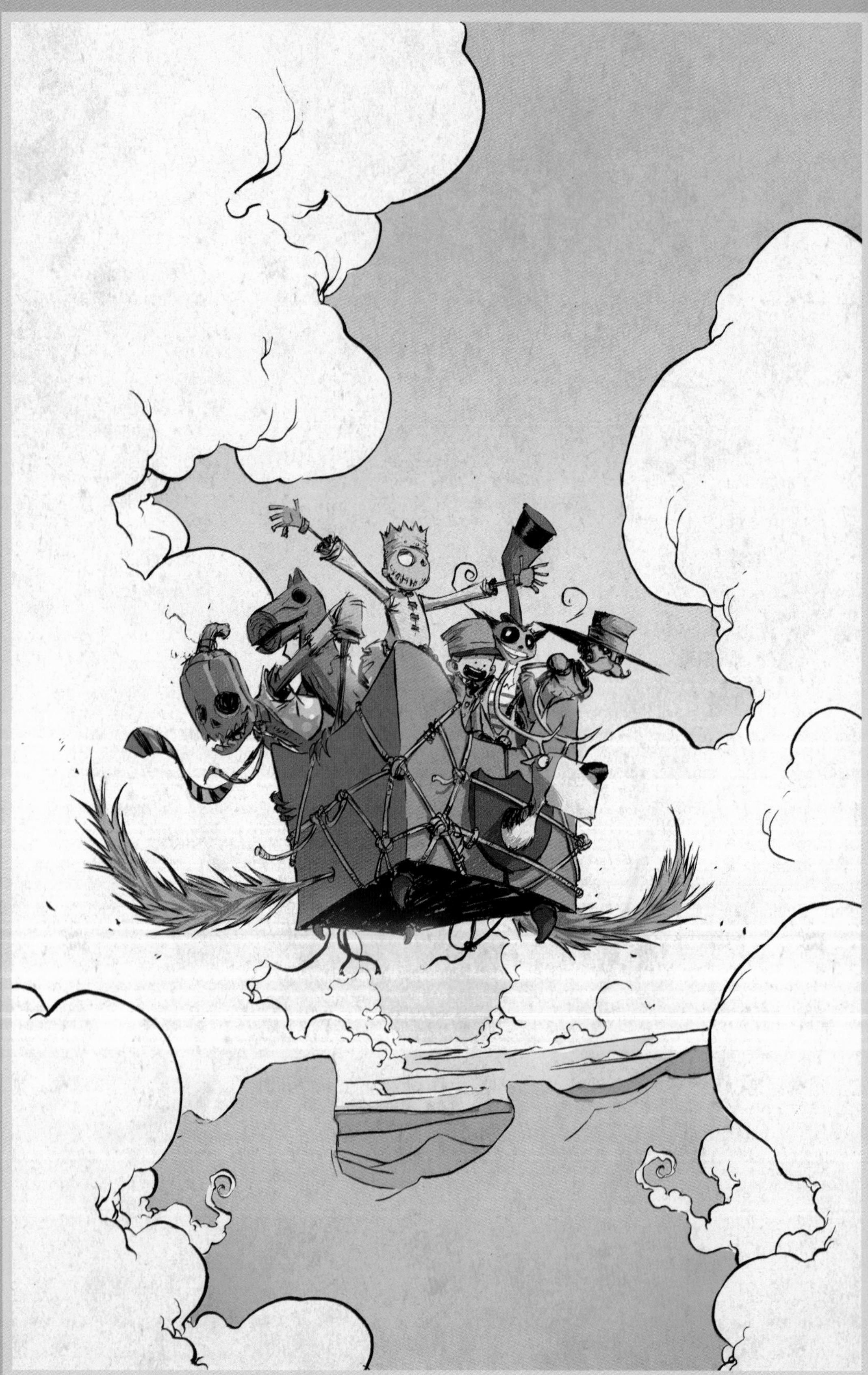

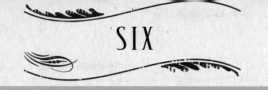

SEVEN

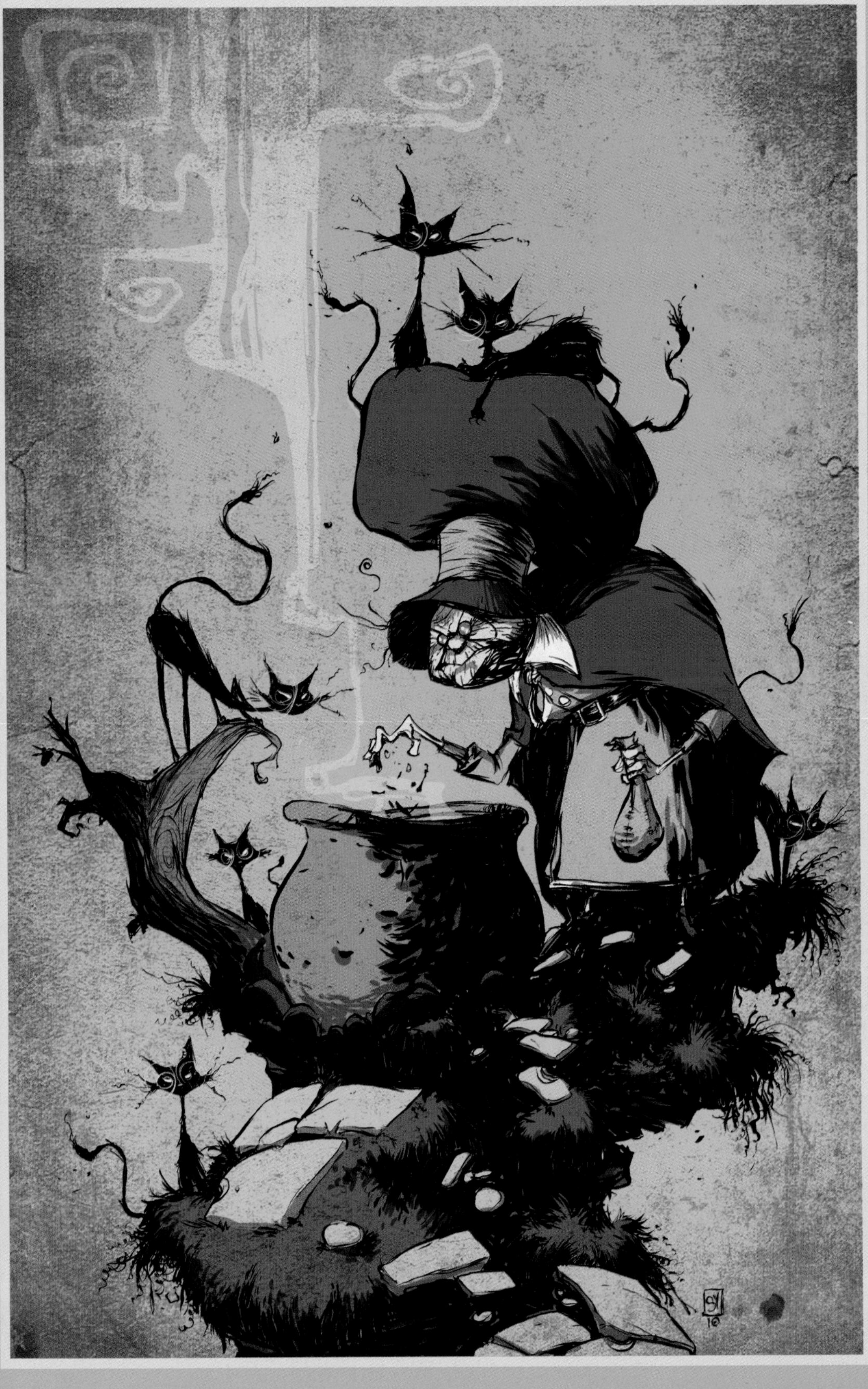

EIGHT

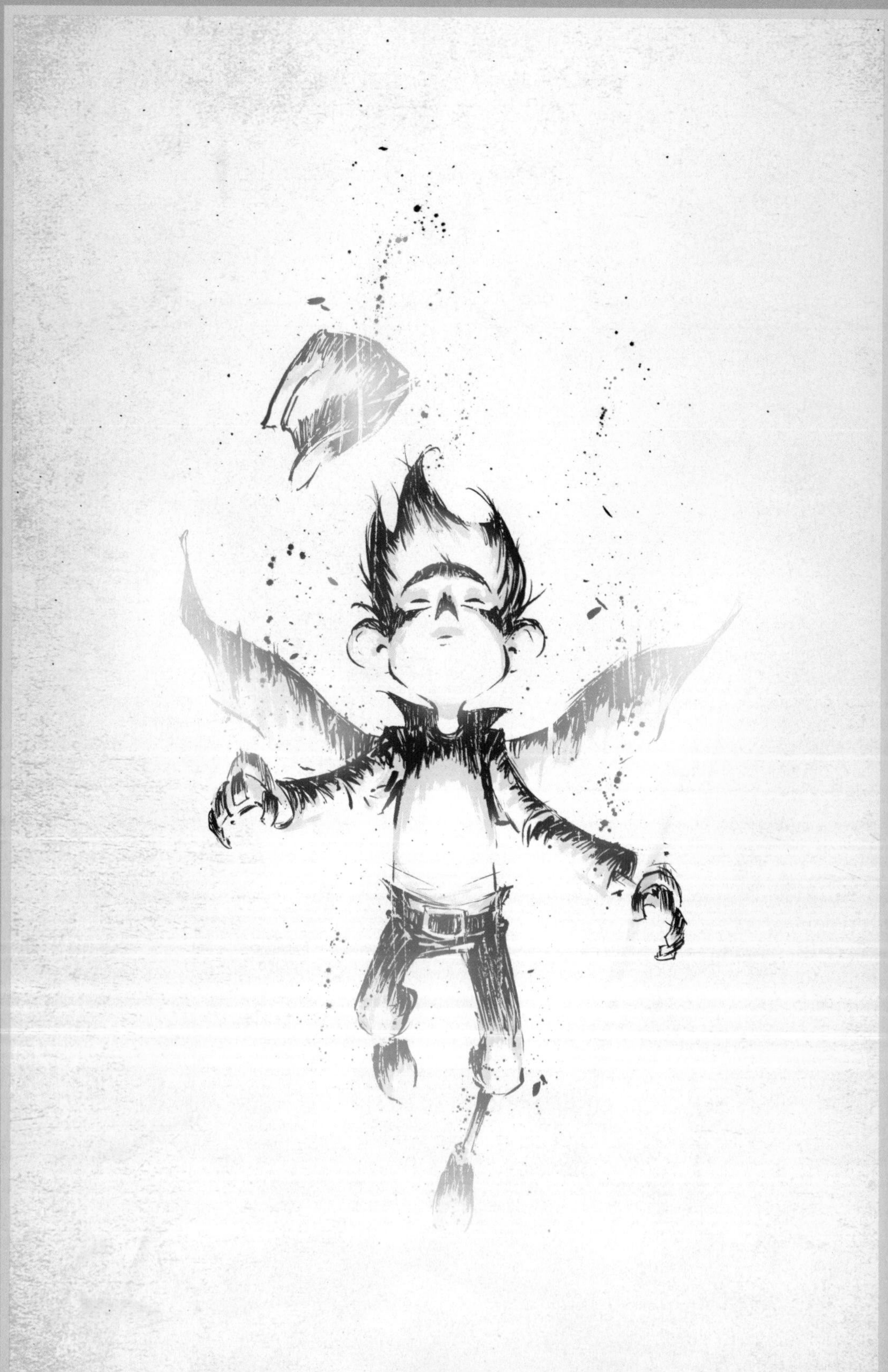

Variant Cover by Eric Shanower

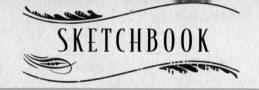

JINJUR

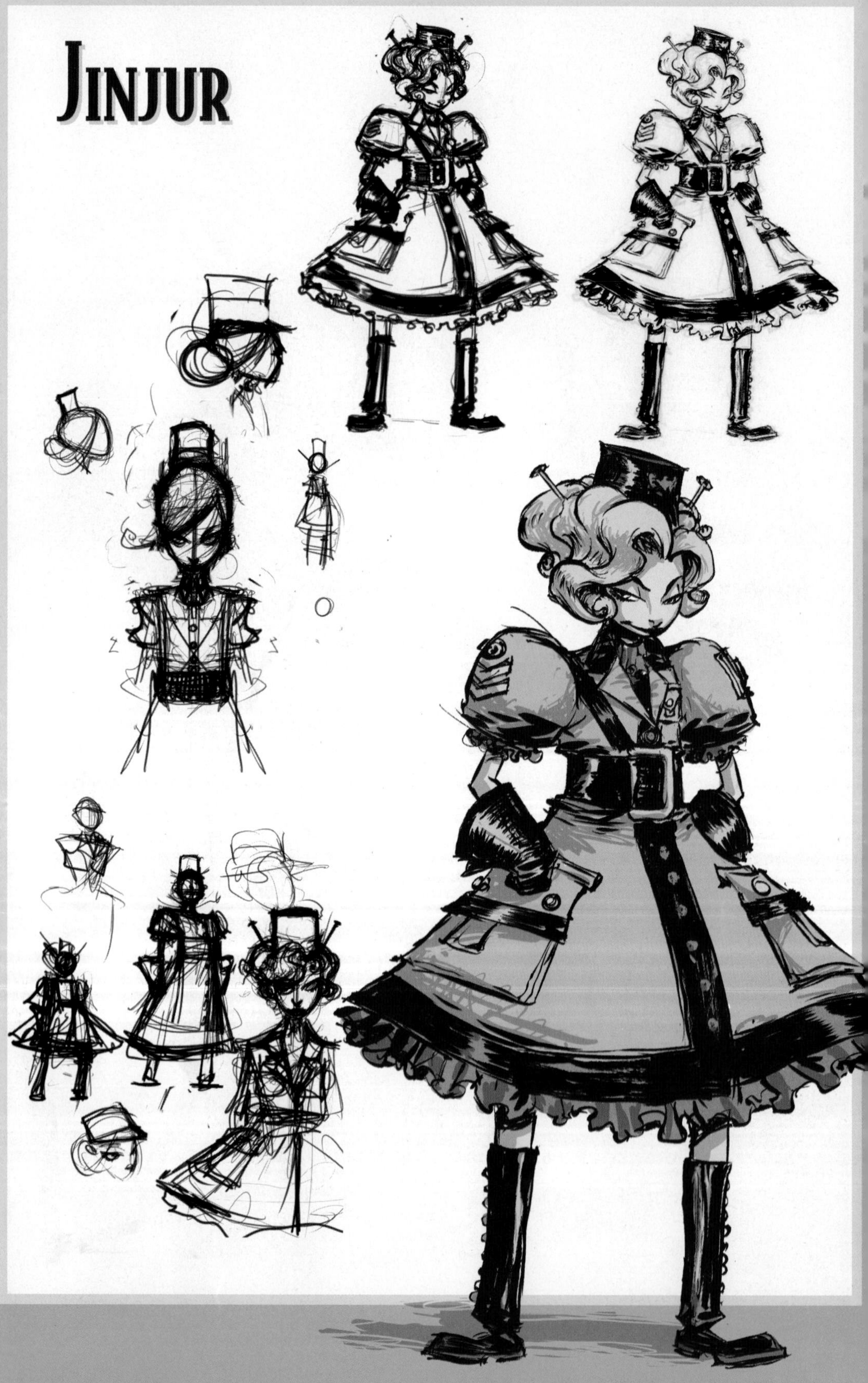

MOMBI

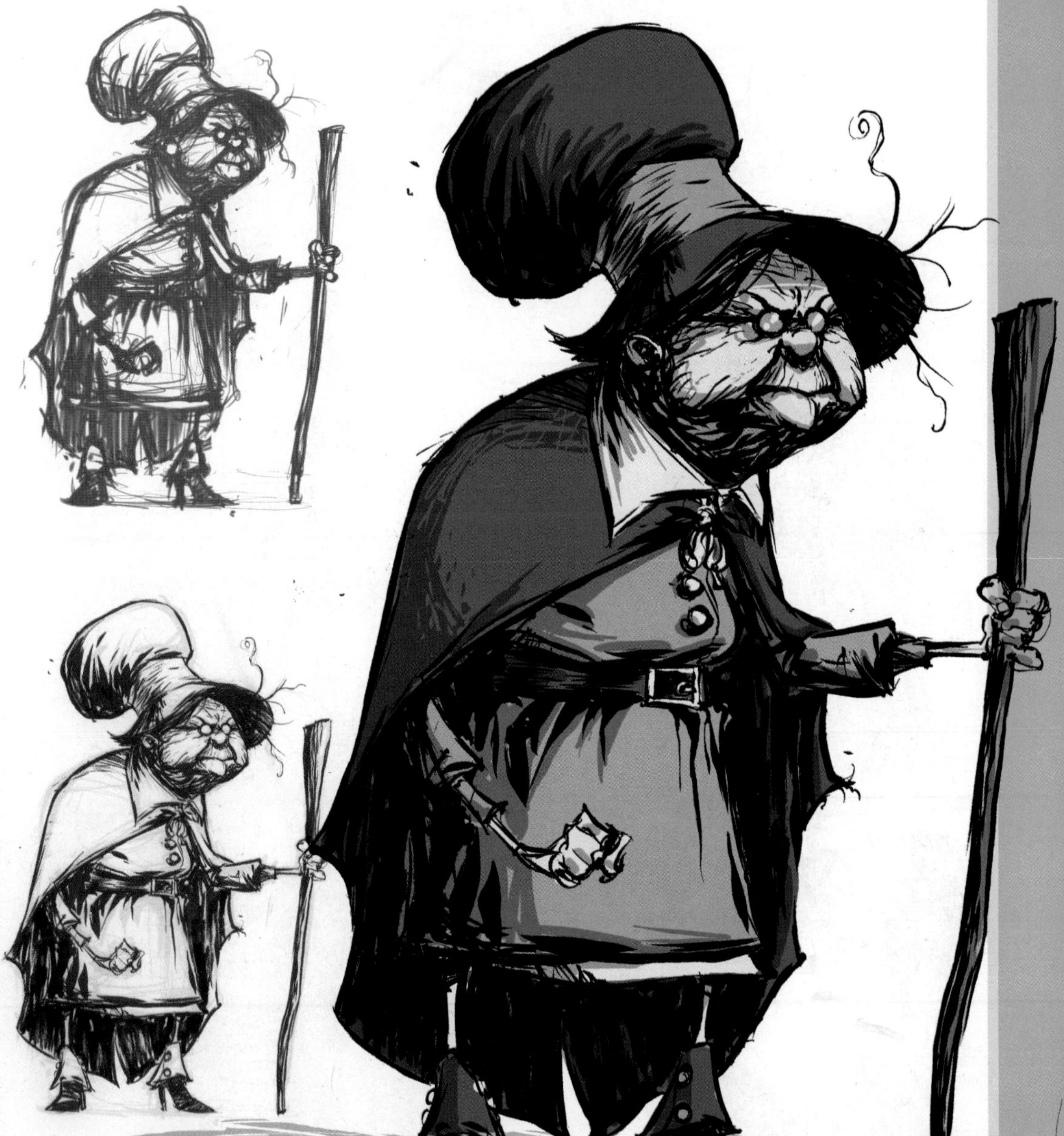

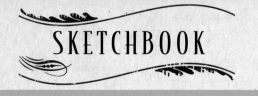

Tip

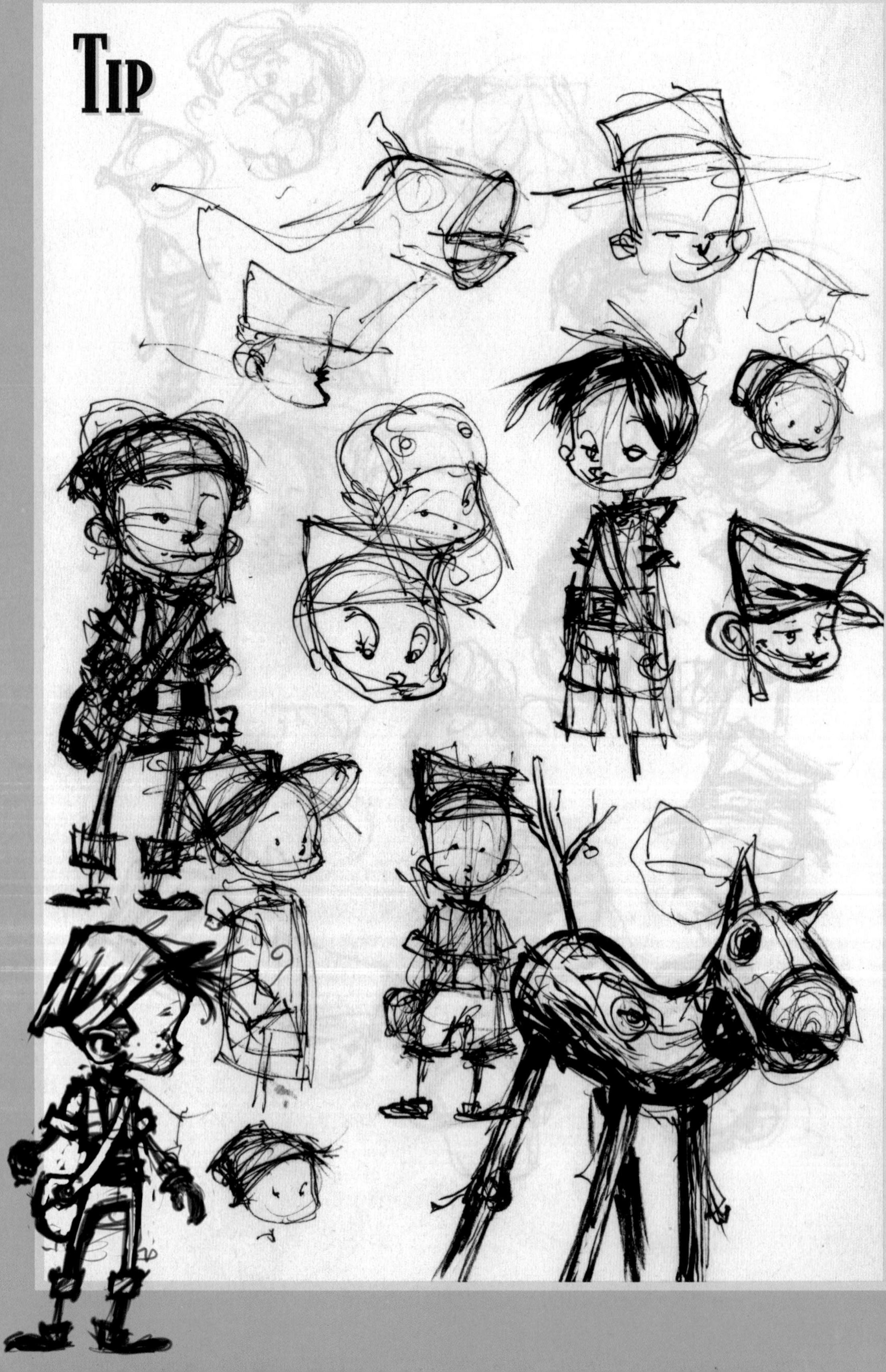

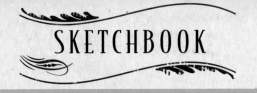

THE WOGGLE-BUG

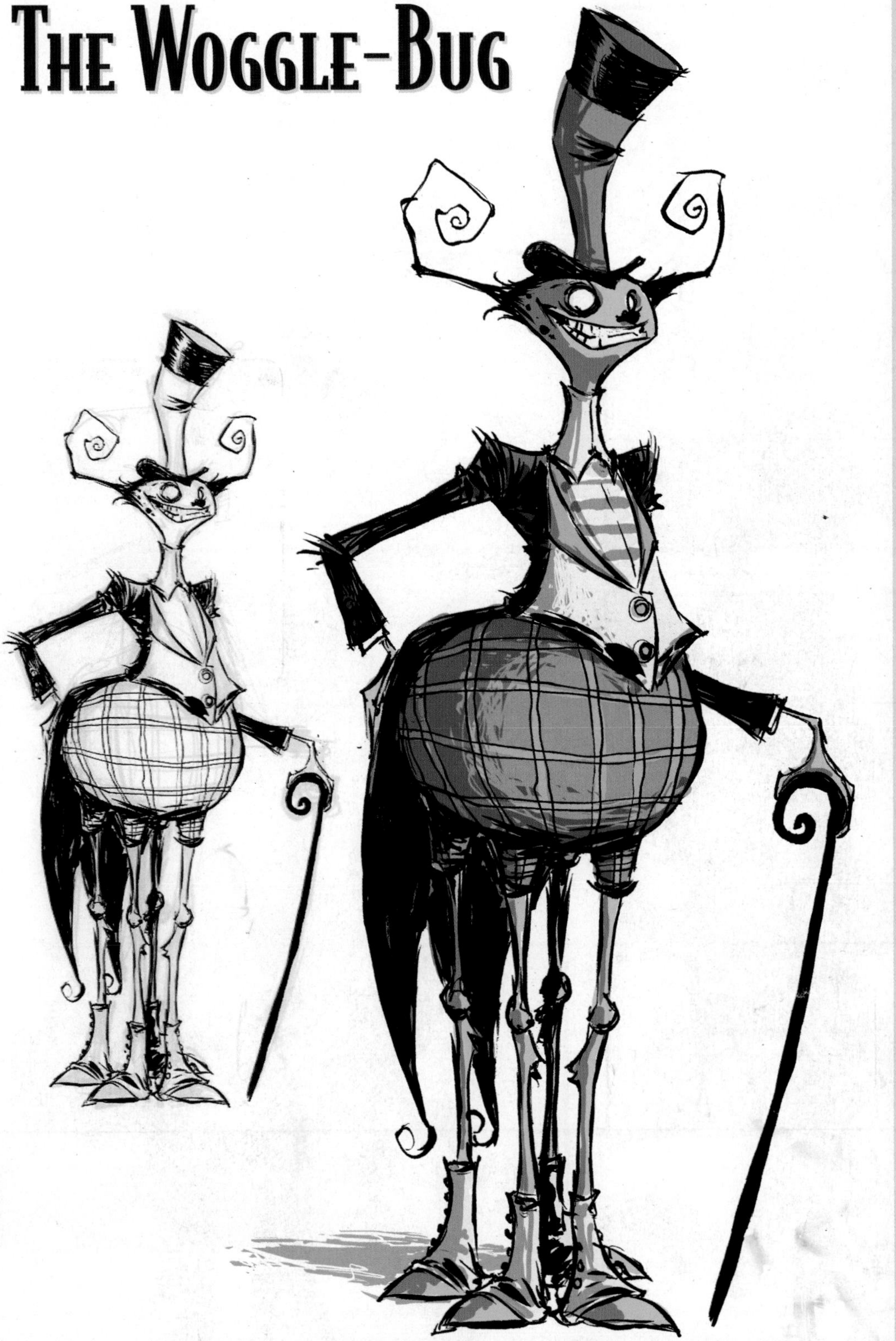

ISSUE ONE COVER PROCESS

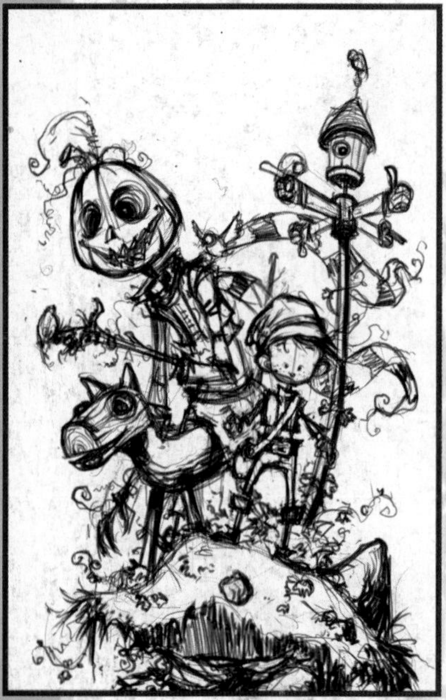

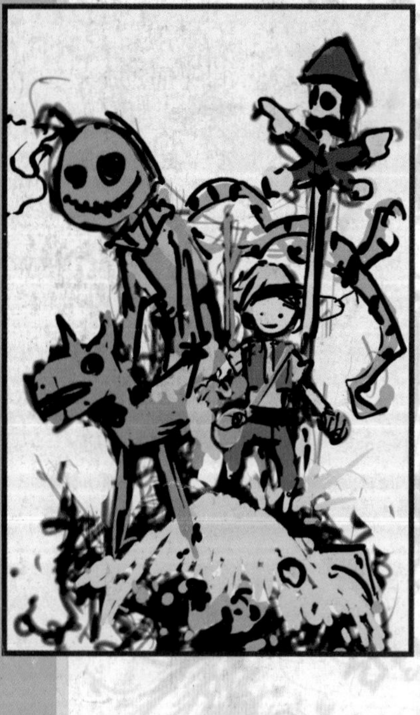

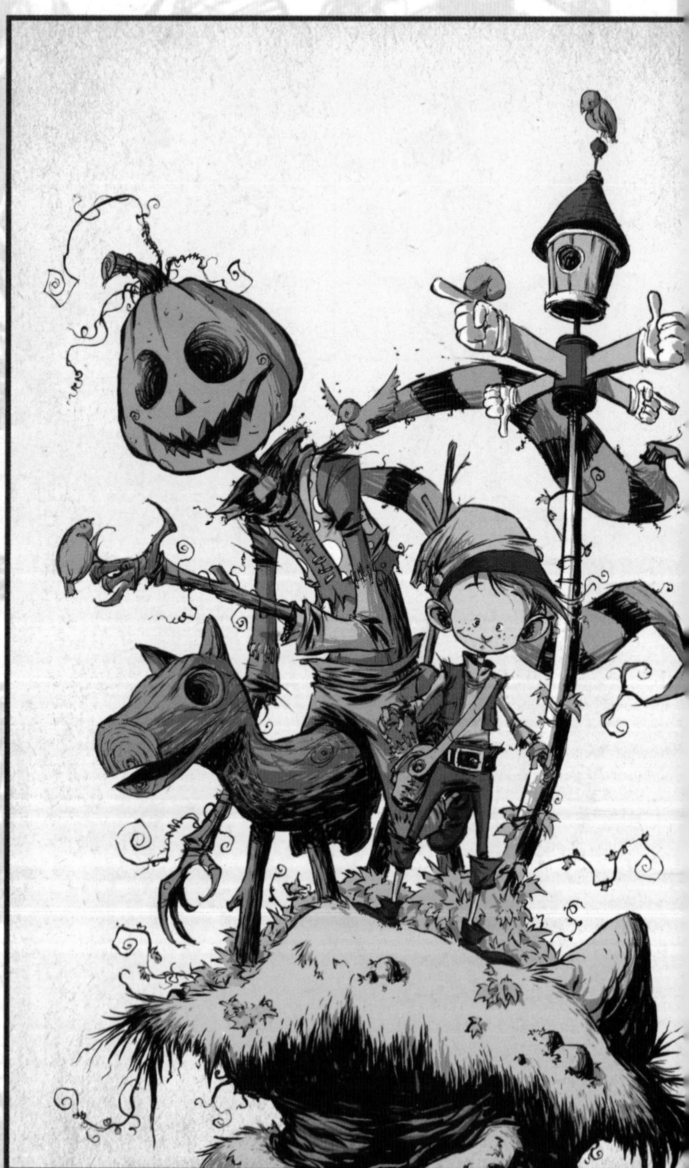

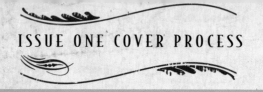